Campfires in Cyberspace

David D. Thornburg, Ph.D.
DThornburg@aol.com
http://www.tcpd.org

Thornburg, David D.
Campfires in Cyberspace

ISBN 0-942207-14-9 (pbk.)
Copyright © 1996 by David D. Thornburg and Starsong
Publications

Published in the United States of America.

ISBN 0-942207-14-9

Dr. Thornburg can be contacted at:
Thornburg Center
P. O. Box 7168
San Carlos, CA 94070
415-508-0314
DThornburg@aol.com

http://www.tcpd.org

Contents

Dedication

This book is dedicated to the memory of my mother and father. My mom was an artist with a deep love of philosophy. While her interests in media overlapped with those of Marshall McLuhan, her personal focus was on the works of Socrates, Plato and Aristotle. She was acutely aware of the impact of media on our lives and was always encouraging me to step carefully through the minefields of educational technology. She encouraged me to think about figure and ground simultaneously — a gift I have tried to honor in this book.

My dad took a more hands-on approach to media. He was a scientist and a photographer. His interests were split between artifact and effect. Like his father, my dad enjoyed new technologies, but had deep reverence for the old. His computer was adjacent to the area where he made gears by hand for the repair of antique clocks — one of his favorite pastimes.

Of all my books, this one most reflects the lessons learned from both my parents. Their passing has created a void that has been filled to some small degree by the joy of writing this modest volume with their spirits on my shoulder.

Mom, Dad, I love you both.

DDT, June, 1999

Preface: Classrooms Without Walls

The following poem, *Classrooms Without Walls*, was written by Marshall McLuhan and was published in *Explorations* in May of 1957. As with much of his writing, it could have been written yesterday.

It's natural today to speak
of "audio and visual aids" to teaching,
for we still think of the book as norm,
of other media as incidental.
We also think of the new media
– press, radio, movies, TV –
as MASS MEDIA
& think of the book
as an individualistic form.

Individualistic because it
isolated the reader in silence &
helped create the Western "I."
Yet it was the first product of
mass production.

With it everybody could have
the same books.

*It was impossible
in medieval times for
different students, different institutions,
to have copies of the same book.
Manuscripts, commentaries, were dictated.
Students memorized.*

*Instruction was almost entirely oral,
done in groups.
Solitary study was reserved for
the advanced scholar.
The first printed books were
"visual aids" to oral instruction.*

*Before the printing press,
the young learned by
listening, watching, doing.
So, until recently, our own
rural children learned the
language & skills of their elders.
Learning took place
outside the classroom.
Only those aiming at professional careers
went to school at all.*

*Today in our cities,
most learning occurs outside the classroom.
The sheer quantity of information conveyed by
press-mags-film-TV-radio*
far exceeds
*the quantity of information conveyed by
school instruction & texts.
This challenge has destroyed
the monopoly of the book as a teaching aid
& cracked the very walls of the classroom,
so suddenly,
we're confused, baffled.*

In this violently upsetting social situation,
many teachers naturally view
the offerings of the new media
as entertainment,
rather than education.
But this view carries
no conviction to the student.
Find a classic
which wasn't first regarded
as light entertainment.
Nearly all vernacular works
were so regarded until the 19th century.

Many movies are obviously handled
with a degree of insight & maturity
at least equal to the level permitted
in today's textbooks.
Olivier's Henry V & Richard III
assemble a wealth of
scholarly & artistic skill
which reveal Shakespeare at a very high level,
yet in a way easy
for the young to enjoy.

The movie is to dramatic representation
what the book was to the manuscript.
It makes available
to many & at many times & places
what otherwise would be restricted
to a few at few times & places.
The movie, like the book,
is a ditto device.
TV shows to 50,000,000 simultaneously.
Some feel that the value
of experiencing a book
is diminished by being extended

to many minds.
This notion is always implicit
in the phrases "mass media," "mass entertainment" –
useless phrases obscuring the fact THAT
English itself
is a mass medium.
Today we're beginning to realize
that the new media aren't just
mechanical gimmicks
for creating worlds of illusion,
but new languages
with new & unique powers of expression.
Historically, the resources of English
have been shaped & expressed in
constantly new & changing ways.
The printing press changed,
not only the quantity of writing,
but the character of language
& the relations between author & public.
Radio, film, TV pushed
written English towards
the spontaneous shifts & freedom of
the spoken idiom.
They aided us in the recovery
of intense awareness of
facial language & bodily gesture.
If these "mass media"
should serve only
to weaken or corrupt
previously achieved levels of
verbal & pictorial culture,
it won't be because
there's anything inherently wrong with them.
It will be because we've failed
to master them as new languages in time
to assimilate them to
our total cultural heritage.

These new developments,
under quiet analytic survey,
point to a basic strategy of culture
for the classroom.
When the printed book first appeared,
it threatened
the oral procedures of teaching, and
created
the classroom as we now know it.
Instead of making
his own text, his own dictionary, his own grammar,
the student started out with these tools.
He could study, not one,
but several languages.
Today these new media
threaten, instead of merely reinforce,
the procedures of this traditional classroom.
It's customary to answer this threat
with denunciations of the unfortunate character &
effect
of movies & TV,
just as the comicbook
was feared & scorned & rejected
from the classroom.
Its good and bad features
in form & content,
when carefully set beside
other kinds of art & narrative,
could have become a major
asset to the teacher.

Where student interest is already
intensely focused
is the natural point
at which to be
in the elucidation of
other problems & interests.

**The educational task
is not only
to provide
basic tools
of perception,
but to develop
judgment & discrimination
with ordinary social experience.**
*Few students ever acquire skill
in analysis of newspapers.
Fewer have any ability to discuss
a movie intelligently.*
To be articulate & discriminating
about ordinary affairs & information
is the mark of an educated man.
It's misleading to suppose
*there's any difference between
education & entertainment.*
This distinction merely relieves people
*of the responsibility of
looking into the matter.*
It's like setting up a distinction between
*didactic & lyric poetry
on the ground that one
teaches, the other pleases.*
However, it's always been true
*that whatever pleases
teaches more effectively.*

Introduction

This is yet another book about educational technology — a topic that has been hotly debated for many years, and is likely to be talked about for many more to come. Unlike many books on the subject, the focus of this one will be on ways to bend and mold existing telematic media (primarily the World Wide Web) into something that meets the fundamental needs of education. As the poem in the preface illustrates, new media have always been judged with jaundiced eyes — especially when applied to education. The Web is no different from other media in this regard, and yet it is strikingly different from other media in its capacity to be used as a learning tool.

Before continuing, there seems to be some confusion in many peoples' minds regarding the Internet and the Web. These words are often used interchangeably. It is important, I think, to understand that they do not refer to the same thing. The Internet is the communication system and protocols over which Web traffic passes. It consists of a set of rules describing how computer-based information gets from one place to another, and these rules are applied to data of all kinds: e-mail, file transfers, Web-based information, and other data types.

The World Wide Web is one of the most popular applications that uses the Internet (eclipsed only by e-mail). Because many people spend the bulk of their Internet time using the Web, it is easy to see how the two concepts might become merged in their minds. In this book, I will try to use the word "Web" to describe only those applications of the Internet that use the World Wide Web protocols, and refer to the Internet when talking about the underlying communication system itself.

This book operates on a few premises:

First, the Web is largely accidental in terms of its appearance. The look and feel of this medium is mostly the result of the thought processes of two groups of people: Tim Berners-Lee at CERN, a basic physics laboratory in Switzerland, and Marc Andreeson and his colleagues at the supercomputer center at the University of Illinois in Urbana. The Web looks the way it does because these two groups had a particular point of view, not because they had conducted extensive research on how an informational space should be navigated. I would argue that the Web might look quite different had it been designed by people with backgrounds in theater and music instead of science and engineering.

It turns out, lack of planning aside, that the Web has proven to be quite a versatile medium, mostly because its design is flexible enough to incorporate new features as they are invented. This, as you will see, will be important to us as we explore ways the Web can be turned into a dynamic educational tool.

Our second premise is that the Web is the most under-hyped technology in history. This makes it very important for us to think carefully about how the Web can be used as a learning tool. It took 38 years for radio to reach fifty million users. Television took thirteen years to reach this level; but (starting from the release of the Mosaic browser) it took the Web only four years to reach this number of users. The Web has become the fastest growing communication technology in history. Now that computers are in more than fifty percent of America's homes, with an estimated 60% of these computers connected to the Web, the reach of this medium is affecting everything from how we get our news to how we make our purchases.

But, while news gathering and electronic commerce are interesting topics, they pale in comparison with the potential impact of the Web in the area of education. We have all heard the clarion call to lifelong education, yet there are few media capable of addressing this task by themselves. I am of the opinion that the Web has the potential to serve as a powerful tool for lifelong learning, but there is some important thinking to be done before rushing headlong into the fray.

The reason for this comprises our third premise — the Web has yet to become a clearly defined medium. Symptoms of this surround us every day. Listen to how people talk about the Web. They talk as if the Web were a library, a museum, a store, a television or radio station, an art gallery, and so on. Based on the numerous ways people describe the Web, two things are clear. First, it is all of the things that are used to describe it and, second, it is none of these things. This apparent paradox will (I hope) be resolved as this book progresses. In the meantime, think about this: We all talk about the telephone, television, radio, and other technologies without confusion. We don't say that the telephone is someone with a really loud voice screaming between cities. We don't talk about television as a theater using the airwaves. These technologies are sufficiently mature to have entered our vocabulary and understanding as media defined within themselves. We no longer need metaphors to define them — they have their own identity.

It is common for new technologies to be defined initially in terms of the technologies they replace. Hence the automobile was once called a horseless carriage. While the metaphor was useful in describing the technology to new users, it was also quite limiting. Early automobiles looked like horseless carriages, not like the automobiles of today. As long as we look to the past for our metaphors, we restrict the capacity of media to acquire their own definition. As Marshall McLuhan was fond of saying, "We look at the present through a rearview mirror. We march backwards into the future." And so it is with the Web, especially the Web as applied to education.

My goal in this book is to examine the intrinsic nature of learning and to see how archetypal learning environments find their parallels in the Web. In the process, we might even find the very "webness" of the Web itself. Whether we find it or not, I am convinced that the potential of this medium will be limited until we transcend the metaphors that, unfortunately, we will have to use as feeble bridges to the future.

As for the broad structure of this book, technology will take a back seat to pedagogy. My goal is for readers to be able to turn the Web into a more powerful educational tool for themselves and for their clients — learners at all ages and backgrounds who will be spending the rest of their lives in a new century. The first several chapters deal with history, and the remaining chapters deal with pathways to the future. Like any author I have my biases and my influences. I am biased in favor of learners, and I am strongly influenced by the ideas of Marshall McLuhan and his mentor, Harold Innis.

And, so, dear reader, let us explore together and, in the process, re-invent the Web to our purposes. As my 1970s Xerox PARC colleague Alan Kay often remarked, the best way to predict the future is to invent it.

Let us invent the future together!

From Metaphors to Artifacts

Ask someone to define the World Wide Web and, most likely, you'll get a response describing many things — a library, a museum, a store, a radio station, a classroom. It seems that there is no way (today) to describe the Web except by reference to other artifacts we already know about.

This is a property of most new technologies. When the steam locomotive was invented, it was called the "iron horse." The automobile was called the "horseless carriage." The computer was called the "electronic brain." And yet none of these artifacts is called by its old name today. In fact, we consider the old names limiting to our definition of the technology. Today we mention trains, automobiles, computers and other devices without having to explain what we are talking about. These words moved into our cultural lexicon as items in themselves, no longer needing descriptors based on metaphors or similes.

Every so often a new artifact comes into existence that defies analogical comparison with what has gone before. Hypertext, a word now understood at a functional level by millions, was once incredibly obscure. The idea that text objects could be linked to other text objects so that, by selecting one part of a document you could be transported to another document or a connected part of the same document, was a strange concept to many. This was especially true for generations brought up on the linear sequential nature of text. With the exception of the "make your own adventure" stories that had readers skip to different parts of the book based on their choice of desired actions, the world of physical documents had little in it to prepare us for the concept of hypertext or hypermedia in general.

When Apple Computer gave away copies of Hypercard, a hypermedia authoring tool, with every Macintosh, they paved the way for increased understanding of this concept. Many learned what hypermedia was by directly experiencing it, not by drawing parallels to other media. While hypertext products were on the market prior to the release of Hypercard, it was the widespread (and free) distribution of this tool that had the greatest effect. One consequence of this is that "hypertext" is generally understood by those who use tools incorporating its features. We skipped the "hypertext as click on some text to jump to some related information" phase. Direct experience obviated the need for an "iron horse."

And yet this has not been our experience with the Web. Even though the Web is about ten years old, we still refer to it in terms of the media types and artifacts it enhances or replaces. Instead of being a single "iron horse," it is several, and the primacy of one over the other is hotly debated. In early 1999, for example, Web search engines decided to become "portals" — launching pads for users' Web experience. A few years before, the hot buzzword was "push" technology that modeled the Web on broadcast media (such as radio and television) that push their content to the user without the user having to do anything to get it.

Perhaps the reason we have not come to a common understanding of the word "Web" is because the Web is constantly changing on us. In the beginning the Web was purely text-based. Next, graphics were added. Now virtually all media types are supported, and one can be sure that new types will be supported as they are invented.

Another reason for relying on old metaphors is that they are comforting. We understand what libraries are, so those who think of the Web as a library are able to use this metaphor as a touchstone in their initial explorations of the medium. It is only after gaining comfort in familiar ground that some people will be willing to venture off that path into new territory.

All of this makes life hard for anyone trying to figure out the intrinsic "webness" of the Web. But even if we decide this task is impossible, I think we need to persevere simply to insure that we are using this artifact to its greatest potential. Nowhere is this more important than in our use of the Web as a learning tool.

The Web has been used for learning since its inception. Scientists could read the work of their colleagues as soon as it was posted, and could create links to their own work, or to the work of others. This process of transforming linear text to hypertext turned annotations from nouns to verbs. Instead of static references to other work, a hypertext annotation takes you to the work itself.

More recently, with the addition of rich media types (including images, sounds, animations, simulations, and the capacity to transmit computer files of all kinds), the Web has found increasing application for learning at all levels, from primary grades through corporate training. Web-based distance learning (primarily offered through intranets) is actively promoted in organizations of all sizes. According to the research firm, IDC, the US-based intranet/internet learning market will grow from about $200 million in 1997 to well over three trillion dollars by 2001. In the K-12 arena, educational Web sites abound, with more being added every day. Teachers and students alike are finding information and connecting with other rich learning resources through this medium. As access in our classrooms grows to catch up with that in homes, and as home access continues to grow, there is little question that the Web increasingly will be applied to learning for all members of the family. Not only does the Web support anywhere/anytime learning, it also supports an audience of one — instructors no longer have to wait until a certain number of students have enrolled to justify the offering of a course.

What is essential, though, is that instructional designers have as clear a grasp as possible of what the Web is and what it can offer to education. Without this big-picture understanding, they risk being one of the proverbial blind men feeling a single part of the elephant and proclaiming that they understand the essence of the whole thing. One might think an elephant is a rope based on feeling the tail, or think it is a tree trunk by feeling a leg, and so on. This short-sighted view results in tremendous misunderstandings whether the topic is the Web, or elephants!

The Tetrad

In Marshall McLuhan's later years he developed a technique for exploring the effect of technology on society. This technique is based on the idea that every artifact (whether physical or conceptual) does four things:

1. It creates something new through enlargement or enhancement.
2. It obsoletes something used prior to the new technology.
3. It retrieves or rekindles something from the past.
4. It flips or reverses into something else when pushed to the limit of its potential.

While the idea of this tetrad started showing up in his lectures, its full exposition took place in a posthumous book he co-authored with his son, Eric, *Laws of Media: The New Science*, and in a book co-authored with Bruce Powers, *The Global Village: Transformations in World Life and Media in the 21st Century* .

The tetrad is a powerful tool for many reasons. First, it forces the user to think clearly about the artifact under study. Second, it addresses past, present and future all at once in a holistic manner, with a resonance of all four aspects existing at one time in a complex relationship between figure and ground. So we have the situation where retrieval is to obsolescence as enhancement is to reversal — what is brought back must render something obsolete; what is enhanced will always do so at the expense of something else. At the same time, retrieval is to enhancement as obsolescence is to reversal. What is retrieved is an outgrowth of the enhancement. What is obsolesced creates the opportunity for reversal.

McLuhan's process for tetrad creation comes from answering these four questions of the artifact under study:

1. What does the artifact enlarge or enhance?
2. What does it erode or obsolesce?
3. What does it retrieve that had been earlier obsolesced?
4. What does it reverse or flip into when pushed to the limits of its potential?

The process of answering these questions reveals the depth of understanding that we have regarding the artifact. If you have a hard time answering these questions, then perhaps the artifact has not matured to the point where it can be understood. Of course, you might understand the artifact itself — especially if it is a physical item like a computer or a telephone. What may lie hidden from view is the affect of the artifact — the ground relationship underneath the artifact as figure. This simultaneous figure/ground relationship of artifacts underpins McLuhan's famous quotation: "The medium is the message."

The following figure shows the four aspects of the tetrad with their relationship to each other. In our examples, we'll work our way around the figure in sequence.

Tetrad

Enhances   Obsoletes

Reverses   Rekindles

To illustrate the process, let's start with desktop publishing.

1. Desktop publishing enhanced the capacity of everyone to become a publisher. This was facilitated by the ease with which attractive page layouts could be created and then printed with laser printers whose image quality approached that of low-end offset presses.

2. Desktop publishing obsoleted the typewriter, paste-up tools, Xacto knives, and page layout tables.

3. Desktop publishing rekindled an interest in typography — an art form that was popular during the Renaissance.

4. As computers became capable of running more powerful desktop publishing software, they kindled an interest in the creation of interactive multimedia — allowing the creation of documents for which there was no printed analog. Publishing

moved from printing to the creation of non-printable documents.

Desktop Publishing

Allows everyone to be a publisher

Obsoletes typewriter, pasteups

Reverses into interactive multimedia

Rekindles interest in typography

To apply the tetrad to the Web in education, we need to identify four things:

1. What is it that the Web enhances in education?
2. What does it obsolete?
3. What does it rekindle from the past?
4. What does it flip into when pushed to the limit?

The rest of this book is devoted to this task.

Before moving to the next chapter, you might want to create a tetrad on this topic yourself. Use each of the four questions as a focal point for conversation. You will probably end up with long lists of answers to each question. This is appropriate, especially since the Web is such a dynamic and fluid medium. I've spent a significant fraction of the past six years trying to answer these questions myself.

The next chapter looks at communication revolutions from a historical perspective. Many of the challenges faced by educational technology enthusiasts have happened before!

From Tribes to Cybernauts

In order to gain insights on the potential impact of the telematic revolution on education, it is valuable to examine what has gone before. Some futurists, like Alvin Toffler, for example, talk about historical epochs in terms of commerce. In his book *The Third Wave*, Toffler describes the move from the agricultural age to the industrial age, and from there to the information age — shifts characterized by transformations in dominant economic forces.

Marshall McLuhan, in *Gutenberg Galaxy* and other writings, proposed an alternative view of historical context: that we are shaped by our dominant modes of communication, and that this has tremendous impact on the economy. This perspective echoes that of Harold Innis, whose book *Empire and Communications* sets the stage for much of McLuhan's work. The contemporary author James O'Donnell expands and elaborates on this theme in his book, *Avatars of the Word: From Papyrus to Cyberspace*.

The personal analysis that follows owes much to these authors. My focus will be on four major modalities of communication and on the stress that resulted as we moved from one to the next over the millennia.

McLuhan popularized the idea that humankind has experienced four stages of development in communication:

Tribal
Scribal
Typographic, and,
Cybernetic

The shift from one to the other was triggered by a major invention that had a transformative impact on society.

Tribal mankind was home to oral tradition. It had a long run, and my use of the word Campfire for the informational space honors at least one of the environments in which the storyteller held court.

Scribal mankind rose to ascendancy after the invention of the phonetic alphabet — a development that McLuhan ranks as one of (if not the) greatest inventions of all time. For the first time, stories could be written down — we could have stories without the storyteller.

Typographic mankind emerged with the popularization of the mass-produced book, starting in the late 1490's. Low-cost books printed on inexpensive paper in the language of the people opened the door to universal literacy.

Cybernetic mankind is in the process of being defined during our time, and had its start in the period between the invention of the telegraph and the computer, but is now just starting to reach its potential in the realm of telematics where computer-mediated access to remote libraries is changing the face of communication once again.

This model of the past and present is, in my opinion, more valuable than the agriculture/industry/information model used by others, especially when talking about education. Educational practice throughout the ages has been shaped by the dominant forms of communication, and the transition from one to the next caused great anxiety among educators of the time.

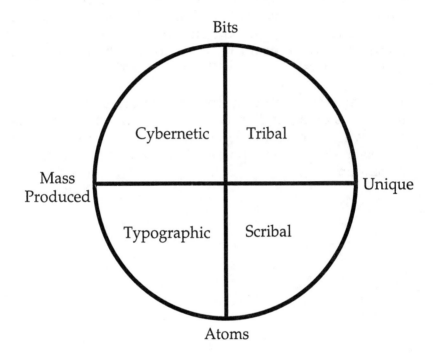

To get a sense of why this is so, I created the figure above in which each communication mode occupies its own quadrant of a circle. The vertical line moves from the world of bits (the non-physical representation of information) on the top, to atoms (information frozen in physical form) at the bottom. The horizontal line moves from uniqueness on the right to mass-production on the left. Each of the four communication modes is typified by a pair of attributes from these lines. For example, the Tribal world was home to the storyteller. Stories in those days had no physical representation, and each telling of the story was unique. With the invention of the phonetic alphabet, stories could be frozen in physical form, but they were still unique because each manuscript was created one at a time by hand. With the popularization of moveable type, frozen stories could be mass-produced. And, now, with the invention of the Web, we have the mass-production of diaphanous information — information once again represented in the non-physical medium of bits.

The challenge of moving from one of these quadrants to the next is great, and an understanding of why this is the case will help, I think, as we continue to seek an understanding of the potential impact of the Web on education.

From tribal to scribal...

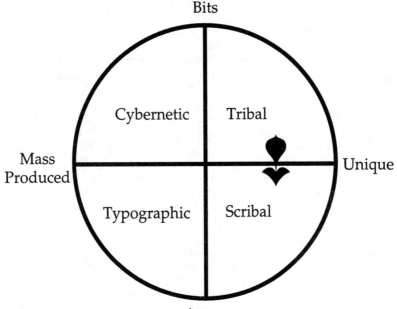

Bits

Cybernetic | Tribal

Mass Produced | Unique

Typographic | Scribal

Atoms

SOCRATES: But there is something yet to be said of propriety and impropriety of writing.

PHAEDRUS: Yes.

SOCRATES: Do you know how you can speak or act about rhetoric in a manner which will be acceptable to God?

PHAEDRUS: No, indeed. Do you?

SOCRATES: I have heard a tradition of the ancients, whether true or not they only know; although if we had found the truth ourselves, do you think that we should care much about the opinions of men?

PHAEDRUS: Your question needs no answer; but I wish that you would tell me what you say that you have heard.

SOCRATES: At the Egyptian city of Naucratis, there was a famous old god, whose name was Theuth; the bird which is called the Ibis is sacred to him, and he was the inventor of many arts, such as arithmetic and calculation and geometry and astronomy and draughts and dice, but his great discovery was the use of letters. Now in those days the god Thamus was the king of the whole country of Egypt; and he dwelt in that great city of Upper Egypt which the Hellenes call Egyptian Thebes, and the god himself is called by them Ammon. To him came Theuth and showed his inventions, desiring that the other Egyptians might be allowed to have the benefit of them; he enumerated them, and Thamus enquired about their several uses, and praised some of them and censured others, as he approved or disapproved of them. It would take a long time to repeat all that Thamus said to Theuth in praise or blame of the various arts. But when they came to letters, This, said Theuth, will make the Egyptians wiser and give them better memories; it is a specific both for the memory and for the wit. Thamus replied: O most ingenious Theuth, the parent or inventor of an art is not always the best judge of the utility or inutility of his own inventions to the users of them. And in this instance, you who are the father of letters, from a paternal love of your own children have been led to attribute to them a quality which they cannot have; for this discovery of yours will create forgetfulness in the learners' souls, because they will not use their memories; they will trust to the external written characters and not remember of themselves. The specific which you have discovered is an aid not to memory, but to reminiscence, and you give your disciples not truth, but only the semblance of truth; they will be hearers of many things and will have learned nothing; they will appear to be omniscient and will generally know nothing; they will be tiresome company, having the show of wisdom without the reality.

Plato, *Phaedrus*

This excerpt from *Phaedrus* shows some measure of Socrates' aversion to writing. (It is, indeed, fortunate that

Plato did not share this aversion since we might not have any surviving copies of Socrates' work otherwise!)

There is no question that the invention of the phonetic alphabet threatened the existing order. In the absence of writing, storytellers determined what was told, and when. Each story was unique and was adapted to the audience. The great legends were elaborated upon over the ages, with changes to the storyline being made as appropriate. The storyteller held great power within the tribe, and Socrates was exemplary in this capacity.

With the rise of the scribal culture, stories could be frozen in time. For the first time, we had stories without the storyteller. This caused a tremendous power shift away from the storyteller to the scribes and the growing (but limited) pool of people who had learned to read and write.

A second challenge to the existing power structure came from the capacity to reflect and then re-read a manuscript. Unlike a story that evaporates upon its telling, the frozen form of the manuscript allowed it to be referenced again and again, and allowed the reflective creation of ancillary texts that explored aspects of the original story in greater depth. The commentaries, sometimes appearing in the margins of the manuscripts, became new stories themselves. It is hard to imagine how this transformation could have taken place without the capacity to have a physical document that could be read and re-read as many times as needed.

The storytellers were threatened for another reason as well. The written form of the story allowed information to be passed in the absence of human contact. The dehumanizing quality of this experience was of great concern to some who felt that true learning could only take place through the personal interaction between two or more people meeting face-to-face.

We perpetuate this concern today every time we ask what will happen when our children spend so much time on-line that they forego their interaction with peers and human teachers. This is not an idle concern. But, just as manuscripts did not replace the need for human teachers, neither will the Web. While we have some people in our culture who prefer the company of books over people, and some who share a similar affection for the world on-line, the bulk of humanity still savors peer interaction, and the millennia since the advent of writing have done nothing to change this.

From scribal to typographic...

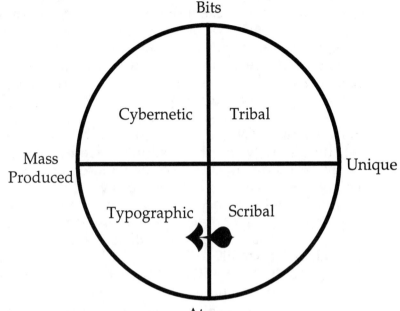

Bits

Cybernetic | Tribal

Mass Produced | Unique

Typographic | Scribal

Atoms

"Pasquedieu! and what kind of books are these you are talking about?"

"There is one of them," said the archdeacon. He threw open his cell window and pointed to the vast church of Notre-Dame, the dark outline of its towers, its stone walls, and immense hip-roof silhouetted against the starry sky, and looking like a gigantic sphinx seated in the middle of the town.

The archdeacon stood for awhile without speaking, contemplating the stupendous edifice. Then with a sigh he pointed with his right hand to the book lying open on the table, and looking sorrowfully from one to the other, "Alas!" he said, "this will kill that!"

Victor Hugo, *The Hunchback of Notre-Dame*

The transition from scribal to typographic mankind came about with the popularization of the mass-produced book. These (relatively) inexpensive volumes were printed on paper in the language of the people. Access to books, once restricted to the privileged few, was, by the late 1490s, available to many. The spread of printed (as opposed to hand-written) books posed several threats to the existing power structure.

First, the monks whose monasteries were kept solvent by the productivity of their scribes, were now facing competition from a new source of manuscripts over which they had no control. The print shops were staffed by new people, and were located in places remote from the cloistered halls. The threat was real. As James O'Donnell states in *Avatars of the Word*, Benedictine monasteries grew quickly from 500 to 1000 C.E., with sustained growth and prosperity up to 1500. However, after the advent of print, monasticism and its allied institutions faded rapidly in the sixteenth century. While a few monasteries attempted to maintain print shops and scriptoria in the same location, the bulk did not.

A second threat to the existing power base was posed by widespread dissemination of the book in education. In the middle ages, teachers were lecturers hired for their clear diction. They would read their copy of a book to students eager to transcribe and make their own copies. An understanding of the content described in the book was not required of the lecturer in this setting.

Once textbooks were readily available in mass-produced form, lecturers needed to be replaced by educators who understood the subject matter and could facilitate student learning in conjunction with the text.

A third threat of the typographic age was the rise of universal literacy. Once books and other text-based documents could be produced cheaply, information became widely available to the masses. This threatened the authority of those who had maintained power by being the arbiters of information. Vestiges of resistance to this power shift can be seen in the school textbooks of today which, in many cases, are published in two formats: one for the student, and another for the teacher. The teacher's edition of the text contains additional material, answers to quizzes and other information that helps maintain the superior knowledge base of the educator. One consequence of this is the perpetuation of a curriculum based on "I've got a secret." As long as the purveyors of textbooks can maintain some semblance of information control in the hands of educators, the typographic revolution is not nearly as threatening as it would be otherwise.

It is no surprise to find that the mass-produced book was actively fought by the scribal community. Just as they had wrenched power from the oral storytellers many centuries before, they were now being eclipsed by the advance of a new technology. In the early days of the typographic revolution, resistance took many forms. As O'Donnell states in *Avatars of the Word,* proponents of the scribal culture were quick to point out the faults of mass-produced books:

1. An error in a printed book was repeated in all copies.
2. The popularization of books would lead to a glut of information.
3. Paper has a short life compared with animal skins, thus reducing the archival value of printed books.
4. The ethos of the monastery and scriptorium would be undermined by the mass-produced book.

These shortcomings were described by many during the mid- to late-1400s, and (with small translations) they reflect the concerns some express about the Web today. For example, numerous criticisms of the Web in education make the following points:

1. An error in a Web site will spread worldwide with a single mouse click.
2. The popularization of the Web would lead to a glut of information.
3. Many Web sites have content with a short life compared with the permanence of books, thus reducing the archival value of the Web.
4. The ethos of the traditional classroom would be undermined by students having unlimited access to the Web.

Without trivializing these concerns, I think it is possible to suggest that, just as we learned to live with them in mass-produced books, we will learn to adapt in the telematic world as well.

From typographic to cybernetic...

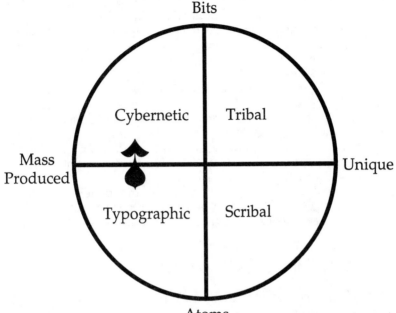

Is it a fact — or have I dreamt it — that, by means of electricity, the world of matter has become a great nerve, vibrating thousands of miles in a breathless point of time? Rather, the round globe is a vast head, a brain, instinct with intelligence! Or, shall we say, it is itself a thought, nothing but thought, and no longer the substance which we deemed it!"

"If you mean the telegraph," said the old gentleman, glancing his eye toward its wire, alongside the rail-track, "it is an excellent thing, — that is, of course, if the speculators in cotton and politics don't get possession of it. A great thing, indeed, sir, particularly as regards the detection of bank-robbers and murderers."

"I don't quite like it, in that point of view," replied Clifford.

"A bank-robber, and what you call a murderer, likewise, has his rights, which men of enlightened humanity and conscience should regard in so much the more liberal spirit, because the bulk of society is prone to controvert their existence. An almost spiritual medium, like the electric telegraph, should be consecrated to high, deep, joyful, and holy missions. Lovers, day by day — hour by hour, if so often moved to do it, — might send their heart-throbs from Maine to Florida, with some such words as these 'I love you forever!' — 'My heart runs over with love!' — 'I love you more than I can!' and, again, at the next message 'I have lived an hour longer, and love you twice as much!' Or, when a good man has departed, his distant friend should be conscious of an electric thrill, as from the world of happy spirits, telling him 'Your dear friend is in bliss!' Or, to an absent husband, should come tidings thus 'An immortal being, of whom you are the father, has this moment come from God!' and immediately its little voice would seem to have reached so far, and to be echoing in his heart.

Nathaniel Hawthorne, *House of the Seven Gables*

While this quotation does not relate specifically to the cybernetic/telematic revolution, it does address many of the same concerns we encounter today. The telegraph was the first technology that separated communication from transportation, and the Web is but the most recent. Enthusiasts and skeptics abound today just as they did in the early days of the electric telegraph.

The transition from typographic to cybernetic mankind is reaching full flower during our lifetime. It is, if McLuhan's model is to be believed, a transition of magnitude equal to that of the invention of the phonetic alphabet or of moveable type. For this reason we should not be surprised that vocal critics of telematics have emerged, especially with regard to the use (or perceived misuse) of these technologies in education. Once again, power is shifted. In this case the primacy of the book-based classroom, where the textbook publisher mediates between the raw source material and the teacher, is threatened when educators and, more importantly, learners can access information from reliable sources directly. The mediation of textbooks in history and science fails to seem relevant when the historical archives of the Library of Congress or the astronomical discoveries of NASA can be revealed with just a few mouse clicks from Web sites that are free to use by anyone with access to the Internet.

The greatest threat to the old order comes from the emerging realization that, in a world overflowing with content, content is no longer king — context is. The old model of teaching as telling falls aside when information is freely available. The telematic educator of the cybernetic age needs to impart different skills to learners: the skills of finding information in a growing sea of material, of determining the relevance of the information found, and of determining the accuracy of this information. These are very different skills than those required in a textbook-driven world where the information in the books is generally accepted without question, even if it is incomplete or, in some cases, wrong.

As with the previous two revolutions in communication, this one threatens the old guard. Some educators have transformed themselves to embrace the new tools, and others actively fight to preserve the previous paradigm, even though their efforts will fail over the long term. Still others stand on the sidelines waiting for some clarification. In the meantime, the children of this age have embraced the telematic tools because they have known no others. For them there is no battle. They are comfortable with technology, even if no one has taken the time to show them how to use it effectively.

But, as with the revolutions that preceded this one, it is a mistake to assume that the old modes of communication will disappear. Mass-produced books will continue to have their place, as will handwritten documents. Stories will still be told as long as people choose to gather around the campfire. While the modern tools of computation and communication will continue to grow in value for education, we will continue to benefit from the older tools as well, not from some sense of nostalgia, but because they are uniquely effective. The challenge for education in any setting — kindergarten through corporate training — is to find the right balance of media types to meet the learning objectives. This dialog is difficult to maintain when advocates and Luddites retreat to their opposing camps. There is no question that technology is not as good a learning tool as its staunchest advocates claim, nor is it nearly so bad as its detractors suggest. As long as the argument remains polarized, the truly effective use of technology in learning will remain a mere promise.

Media: Hot and Cool

In our quest to find the "webness" of the Web, this chapter will focus on one thing the Web most clearly is not. The Web is *not* television.

Marshall McLuhan made distinctions between media that were "hot" and media that were "cool." His use of these words was derived from their use in music. Big band jazz surrounded your senses and was hot. Improvisational jazz demanded the attention of the listener and was cool. In his attempt to elucidate the qualities of high definition and low definition media, McLuhan applied hot and cool as descriptors. For example, movies surround the viewer with high-definition images and sounds. The viewer is passive recipient in that there is no effort needed to fill in the images. Motion pictures, to McLuhan, were hot. Television, on the other hand, was a cool medium. In McLuhan's time televisions were mostly black and white, had small screens and produced fairly fuzzy images with noticeable scan lines. A show was broadcast at a specific time and, prior to the invention of the VCR, the viewer had to adjust his or her schedule to accommodate the medium. This distinction helped him explain why movies were completely unlike television. Television required more viewer participation and, as a low definition medium, was decidedly cool.

But, if we look at television today, it has matured as a medium and has flipped from cool to hot. Big screen television with high definition images and stereo surround sound has heated this medium to the boiling point. VCRs allow you to see a program when you wish, not limited by the constraints of when it was originally broadcast. In contrast, we now have a new cool medium — the Web.

If you think the distinction is academic, consider this. All attempts to create interactive television have failed in the marketplace. Interactive television is an oxymoron. People do not watch television to interact, and — the "hotness" of the medium precludes it. On the other hand, on the Web, nothing happens without user interaction. We "watch" TV but we "surf" the Web. The Web is the coolest medium around.

This raises some serious questions about WebTV — a technology that was supposed to bring the Web to the huddled masses who, as yet, have failed to grasp the need to add a home computer to the den. The thought behind this product was that, since most people already have televisions and telephones, a small box connecting the two through a Web browser would bring the miracle of the Internet to millions. While the jury remains out on the future of this device, its initial impact has been underwhelming. The reasons for this have little to do with the technology *per se*. It is true that televisions make lousy display devices for text, an expressive form that still dominates the Web. But the biggest challenge faced by WebTV has to do with people's expectations. When someone sits in front of a television, interaction is largely a matter of channel flipping, and the viewer's goal is to be entertained, not to actively participate in the experience. When we watch television, we lean back.

In contrast, the Web is all about interactivity. Nothing happens until we click the mouse. Every page is filled with links that take us to remote destinations in leaps that accumulate complexity exponentially. When we use the Web, we lean in.

The distinction between lean-in vs. lean-back experiences is important. Television is designed to be viewed from an impersonal distance of six feet. The Web is designed to be viewed from a personal distance of twelve inches. When we watch television we stand apart from the crowd. When we use the Web we are at the distance associated with conversation with close friends. Failure to understand this distinction can bring disaster to those who bet on the wrong technology.

To help us understand the Web as an educational tool, the next chapter explores four learning spaces, all needed to create an educational system.

Campfires, Watering Holes, Caves and Life

It was during a hot and humid spell in the early 1990s when I found myself in Washington, D. C., for the purpose of attending an educational technology conference being hosted at the National Academy of Sciences. When the invitation had arrived a few weeks before, I knew that this was a conference I needed to attend simply on the basis of the diverse (and famous) presenters who had been selected. Senators and science fiction authors shared the podium with leaders from education and industry. The presenters were all "picture cards," any one of whom would have attracted people to a conference had he or she been the only presenter in attendance. And so, in the midst of the insufferable heat and humidity of our nation's capital, about 500 or so invited attendees were crowded into the main auditorium of the Academy's distinctive building to take part in one of the finest gatherings of diverse experts ever assembled.

As for the attendees, many of them were of similar caliber to the presenters. Corporate executives, world-class educators, senators, reprasentatives, staff members from the White House, the Department of Education, Department of Labor, Department of Commerce and other agencies were all visibly in attendance. This was to be a very intense learning experience!

A quick scan of the program convinced me that I needed to get a seat early, and that nothing would budge me from my perch until the presentations were over. Author Arthur C. Clarke shared his perspectives on the future live from Sri Lanka by a two-way videoconference. Mitch Kapor used similar technology to interact with us from the Great Wall of China after finding that his flight to the United States would not arrive in time. As each expert took the podium, I sat with my tape recorder and laptop computer ready to capture the insights of these wonderful speakers.

And then a funny thing happened.

About two hours into the presentation, people started to leave the auditorium and mingle in the hallway outside. The challenge of getting so many world-class presenters into a two-day conference had caused the organizers to abandon scheduled breaks, except for lunch and dinner. And, even though these attendees were missing some wonderful presentations, they found it necessary to leave the room for a while. From my vantage point, I could see small clusters of people gathered outside the auditorium. Instead of coming back inside to hear more presentations, many of them were talking with each other as if they needed to process what they had heard before receiving any more information.

That night I thought about this interesting behavior and I then had an insight that has altered my thinking about education ever since: Learning takes place in multiple environments, and if any of these environments is out of balance, learning suffers and people will do something to try to restore the balance themselves. Furthermore, these learning environments (or their archetypes) have always existed, suggesting that we are somehow pre-wired to learn through these modalities in balance with each other.

In thinking about how humans have probably always learned, I identified three primordial learning environments: Campfires, Watering Holes, and Caves.

Campfires are informational spaces where we go to get information from experts. In the past these were the storytellers and shamans who carried the wisdom of the people and shared it in formal settings when it was appropriate to do so. In modern context, our Campfires have become the formal presentations given in classrooms or from the podium at conferences.

Watering holes are conversational spaces where we go to share what we have learned with our peers. This environment is essential because the process of sharing what we have learned gives us the opportunity to test our understanding with others who are going through a similar experience. In modern context, our Watering Holes have become the conversational spaces in hallways, around the water cooler, or copying machine, or in any other area where people congregate and share their ideas with peers. When I taught at Stanford, my students and I would often go to a bookstore/coffee house after class to continue our conversation around the ideas explored in the classroom. Watering holes are often informal in nature (insofar as their conversational nature is concerned) but this might be because we haven't thought about them enough to create them intentionally.

Caves are conceptual spaces where we go to reflect and elaborate in private on what we have learned. Our Caves can be isolated places, or environments filled with the tools of creativity that we need to develop and extend our understanding of what we are learning. Caves are places of reflection, but are also places of invention and discovery.

Armed with this insight, I immediately applied it to the conference I was attending. The conference stressed Campfires to the exclusion of all else. The conference program featured the formal presentations, and, like moths attracted to the flame, several hundred of us had converged to this location to receive insights from these luminaries. While Campfires are effective tools of attraction, a productive learning experience requires more.

The schools of my youth were heavily biased toward the Campfire. Watering Hole and Cave time was left up to the students to find on their own — especially by the time we entered high-school with its heavy emphasis on lecture-based instruction. But, just because something is popular (lectures) does not make it right. We learn however we learn, and the arbitrary imposition of schedules and teaching methodologies cannot overcome eons of experience.

Think for a moment about your own experience attending a conference. Most likely, you were attracted (as am I) by the flame of the Campfire — the descriptions of the wonderful presenters that will be sharing their ideas. And yet, when you attend the conference, do you sit through every presentation you can conceivably attend? Most likely you take a break from presentations to go to the exhibit hall or to mingle with friends. In either case, you have replaced the Campfire with the Watering Hole because you needed to stop getting new information and start sharing what you have heard with others.

In the evening, when you go home or go to your hotel room, do you keep on talking, or do you take some "quiet time" to reflect on the events of the day? Again, most likely, you'll take some time just to be alone with your thoughts either to reflect on what you learned, or to start working on how you plan to apply the things you learned about during the day.

I've had the pleasure of sharing the idea of Campfires, Watering Holes and Caves with thousands of people in the past few years, and felt I was well on the way to developing an understanding of natural learning environments that could be applied across all ages and learning situations.

That was soon to change.

Among others, I shared my ideas with a good friend, Prasad Kaipa. Prasad listened intently and then reflected for a moment. He did not disagree with the basic idea, but felt there was something missing — a fundamental building block that kept the theory from being whole. On reflection he suggested that the missing component was Life — the contextual element of application. Unless your learning is applied, it is sterile. It lacks meaning and will be transitory.   True learning is not just about mastering content; it is about understanding and applying your learning in context. Without the contextual realm, the remaining three environments do not make any sense.

So, instead of a triangle, we now have a tetrahedron — a rigid solid with four corners and four faces. Each triangular face reflects a triad whose opposite pole provides the balancing element of completion. Prasad refers to the process of tetrahedral construction as "thinking in three dimensions," and he has been refining this process for over a decade (http://www.mithya.com).

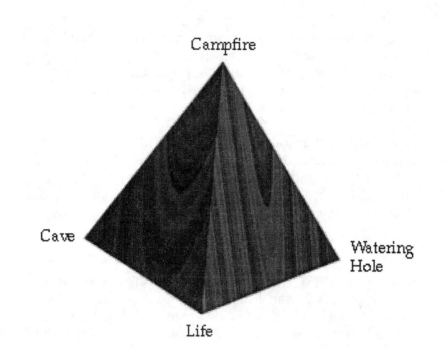

Campfire

Cave

Watering Hole

Life

Just as Life is the balancing element of Campfires, Watering Holes and Caves, we have other balancing relationships as well:

- Campfires balance Life, Watering Holes and Caves
- Watering Holes balance Life, Campfires and Caves
- Caves balance Life, Campfires and Watering Holes

If any part is missing, the tetrahedral structure collapses to a triangle. Any educational setting that fails to embody all four of these basic elements similarly collapses.

The beauty of this theory is that it applies to all learning environments. To be effective, a learning environment of any sort (physical or virtual) needs to have a balance of the following four elements:

1. The informational space of the Campfire
2. The conversational space of the Watering Hole
3. The conceptual space of the Cave
4. The contextual space of Life

What is the proper balance between the four spaces? I don't think there is a rigid answer to this question. My feeling is that learners will move between these spaces at will, based on their own needs at the time. There is no prescribed sequence or preferred ratio of time spent in one space or the other. The only thing I am sure of is that, if one of these environments is missing, learning will suffer. To see why this is so, let's explore the tetrahedron in more depth.

A tetrahedron has four corners, six edges, and four faces. Insights about education can be found by looking at each of these elements by themselves, and then assembling them into a complete figure.

The Four Corners

 The Campfire
In the context of this book, the Campfire is the informational space — the place where we gather, not to converse, but to hear from the teacher. While we might also gather around the fire to tell stories to each other, that activity is relegated (in our system) to the Watering Hole. The Campfire may take different forms in various cultures, but humans have always had special places where they congregated to hear from the experts,

whether they were shamans, teachers, or other people charged with the responsibility of imparting their wisdom to others.

In a traditional school, the Campfire is the classroom. A typical classroom (especially at the upper grades) is set up with the students facing the front of the room. Standing before a blackboard, the teacher is sometimes elevated on a stage to establish superiority. The relationship is clear: except when specifically invited to ask questions or make comments, the student is expected to sit and learn from a lecture. This same room layout is found at conferences, as well as in churches. The flow of information in the Campfire is largely one way.

This layout of the informational space is efficient. A large number of people can listen to a lecture at the same time. College classes sometimes have several hundred students in an auditorium for the lectures, making very efficient use of the instructor's time.

While lectures can be effective tools for imparting knowledge, they are incomplete learning environments. Students inundated with lectures will suffer information overload unless they are given the chance to experience the other learning environments.

The Watering Hole

The Watering Hole is the archetype of a conversational space: a place where peers share ideas with each other. In cultures where water is gathered from a central location, these places are natural points for congregation. As we gather to collect water, we also collect the news from our colleagues. What is new in their life? What have they learned lately?

In modern cultures, the Watering Hole takes many forms. It can be the water cooler at work (or the copying machine, for that matter). It can be a local coffee house or lunchroom. It can be (and is) any place where people congregate in relative quiet to share their thoughts with others. At conferences, spontaneous Watering Holes emerge in the hallways or at the bar. They emerge in exhibit halls. This is one reason why people who attend conferences often skip sessions (Campfires) to talk with friends (Watering Holes) — they need to enter the conversational space to help make sense of what they have heard in the formal presentations.

Watering Holes are so important that some architects have designed them into office buildings. When the Xerox Palo Alto Research Center was designed, alcoves were placed in hallways and couches were placed there to provide comfortable locations where researchers could share their ideas in an informal setting. When I worked there in the 1970s, much cross-fertilization of ideas took place in these spaces. By the same token, our in-house cafeteria employed an excellent chef to entice us to stay on campus during lunch, fostering even more Watering Hole experiences.

 The Cave

The Cave is the archetype of the conceptual space: a place where we go to internalize our knowledge, often giving birth to new expressions of what we have learned. In some cultures, the Cave is a place of quiet reflection where insights are revealed through visions or dreams. The creative process is given free-reign in Caves, no matter what form they take.

Many people need to have "quiet time" during their day just to reflect on the events that have taken place in their lives. For some the Cave might be seat at a kitchen table overlooking a colorful garden. For others it might be a solitary walk in the woods. I have special quiet places where I go to reflect on my life, and you probably do as well.

Cave experiences can be enhanced with suitable tools for creative expression. I carry a variety of tools with me into my Cave: word processors, graphic tools, an audio recorder — all tools designed to let me capture whatever insights I get during this experience. A lot of learning takes place in Caves, even though there is no directed or informal sharing of information with others. The Cave is the place where information is turned into knowledge, and where knowledge can be turned into wisdom.

A digression on creativity

Creativity shifts as we move around the sequence from Campfire, to Watering Hole, to Cave. In the Campfire environment, the storyteller has the creative power and the audience is the (comparatively) passive recipient. Information imparted during this experience might become the impetus for future creative expressions, but, from the perspective of the participant, creative expression does not emerge at this point.

In traditional media, television has emerged as the dominant Campfire in most homes. Viewers sit entranced before the screen, incapable of conversing with the storyteller.

Once you have entered the Watering Hole you are free to share ideas with others and your creative expressions can start to emerge. Many people who have strong interpersonal intelligence can be quite creative in this setting. In the process of sharing ideas with others, they discover their own thoughts. Their colleagues become co-creators in the process and the synergy of interpersonal communication can lead to profound insights for some people.

Every so often I eat at a restaurant that uses paper tablecloths and provides boxes of crayons for diners to use during their conversations with dining mates. It is a delight to watch formally-dressed business people sketching their ideas and sharing them with others and then, when the meal is over, carefully taking their tablecloth with them — perhaps holding the nucleus of a new company in its rough crayon scribblings.

In traditional media, telephones have become electronic Watering Holes — places where ideas can be shared with others in remote locations without having to move our bodies. In fact, when we use the telephone, it is as if we don't have a body — our ideas can be expressed as pure auditory expressions.

It is in the Cave, however, where creativity can find full expression for many people. Removed from distractions of any kind, the Cave-dweller can move into a state of "flow," a place that the social scientist Mihaly Csikszentmihalyi, author of *Creativity: Flow and the Psychology of Discovery and Invention*, says has many attributes, including:

- Immediate feedback — you know right away how you are doing.
- Balance between challenge and skill — your abilities feel matched to the challenges of your actions.

- Action and awareness are merged — your concentration is focused on the current task, not on events of the past or tasks for the future.
- Distractions are excluded from consciousness — you are only aware of what is relevant now.
- No fear of failure — in fact, you feel in total control.
- Self-consciousness disappears — you have no fear of what others may think of your ideas.
- The activity becomes autotelic — you are doing the task because it is intrinsically enjoyable, not for some external reward.
- Sense of time is distorted — hours may pass in what seems like minutes.

This last characteristic of flow — the loss of the sense of passing time — is antithetical to traditional educational environments. Once you have entered the flow state, you can spend hours on a task and yet feel as if only minutes have elapsed. In a classroom setting there are constant distractions, including bells announcing the need to stop whatever you are doing and to start doing something else. Traditional schools are structurally antithetical to creativity for this reason alone.

Each of us has our own triggers for flow. One of mine (that might feel strange for some readers) is working with a computer program that generates incredibly complex fractal images. I can spend hours working with this program, totally oblivious to the world around me. And it is often during the creation of these images that I gain insights that relate directly to a project I am working on. These images become, perhaps, a focusing point for my creative process.

Electronic tools, such as computers equipped with a variety of software packages, can facilitate the Cave experience. For this reason, computer use differs tremendously from television experience. When we view television, we are engaged in a passive lean-back experience. When we use computers, we are engaged in an active lean-in experience. This fundamental difference in media use is significant, even though the display screens might look similar. It is the difference in the use of these two tools that has probably accounted for the failure (so far) of the oxymoronic concept of "interactive television." Television is about receiving information, computers are about creating it. These two activities are practically polar opposites.

As wonderful and as essential as the creative process is, it is only through its application that we make a difference in the world. This brings us to the final corner of the tetrahedron.

 Life

Life represents the contextual space in which our knowledge is applied: the marketplace for ideas and creations of our intellect and effort. Without application, knowledge is hollow.

Much of educational practice in the past was focused on the idea that "content is king." This model is perpetuated today in popular television game shows like Jeopardy where contestants are rewarded for their capacity to recall disconnected and decontextualized fragments of information on demand. The rapid growth of information and information access is rendering the information-delivery model of education obsolete. Content is no longer king; it is free and abundant to the point of overload. Some have argued that we have far too much information available to us today. Against this backdrop it seems strange that many educators still see themselves in the information delivery business. They miss the point. Content is not king; context is king.

Learning is contextual when it is applied to a larger task by the learner. In this space no one asks "Why do I have to learn this?" The question does not come up because the context is clear before the learning takes place. Virtually all learning outside the classroom takes place contextually. The issue is not what is learned as much as it is the timing for the learning. In the contextual space of Life learning takes place just in time to be used, not just in case it will be needed later.

This distinction between Just-in-Time and Just-in-Case learning is a defining feature of the contextual space of Life. For many of my generation our schools seemed devoid of context and we were taught things just in case we needed them later. For example, most of us were taught how to extract the square root of arbitrarily large integers by hand, even though I have yet to find anyone today who needs this skill. This does not mean that there are not things we learn at an early age that have meaning for us later in life. I would argue that literacy, numeracy and an understanding of history and society are foundational components of an educated person. Yet even these are ripe with opportunities for contextual learning. This topic will be explored in more depth later in this chapter.

Another important component of contextual learning has to do with the balance between rigor and relevance. The traditional curriculum in most schools is designed to be rigorous, encompassing everything from learning information to the development of higher-order thinking skills. This characteristic of schooling in the United States is quite positive, but it is not enough. Other countries (including Japan, according to Bill Daggett) have stressed relevance over rigor. Low levels of relevance have to do with knowing information, and high levels of relevance have to do with applying your knowledge to real-world problems that have never been solved before. While rigor and relevance are both of value, neither is complete in itself. The demands of modern society are for people who have high levels of both. If the traditional curriculum covers the rigor axis, it is the contextual domain of Life where the relevance axis shows its strength.

While each of these four corners of the tetrahedron is essential in any learning environment, none is sufficient in itself. In the next section we'll move from the four corners to the six edges: the six unique pairs of attributes that further define learning.

The Six Edges (Diads)

Campfire ↔ Watering Hole
The edge containing Campfires and Watering Holes represents the interaction between information and conversation. I remember times in college when I'd gather with some classmates in the student union to talk about a lecture we'd just heard, but didn't understand. These informal sessions were quite valuable in helping us figure out what the lecturer was talking about. We could compare notes and recollections of what was said, and, more often than not, we'd leave for our next class with a greater awareness of the subject, even though no new information was presented.

Traditional class schedules that move students from room to room with no time for peer interaction make this type of learning impossible. The real benefit comes, I think, when students can interact with each other informally while the presentation is still fresh in their minds. If the interaction is delayed until later in the day, after numerous other presentations, recollections of what was said will have dimmed, and the chance for peer-mediated understanding will be diminished.

Campfire ↔ Cave

The edge containing Campfires and Caves represents the interaction between information and reflection. In some sense these spaces involve solitude. You do not interact during a formal lecture, and in the Cave you are reflecting by yourself. Strongly intrapersonal learners can benefit from having quiet time right after a lecture to collect their thoughts and reframe ideas in their own ways.

In extreme cases, this edge becomes home to Skinnerian stimulus/response models of education in which a fragment of information is presented and is then immediately tested to be sure it has been memorized. No interaction or expansion of the content is possible without feedback, and since the feedback is constrained by the structure of the lesson, this pedagogical model lacks the effectiveness of one that honors dialogue on the topic being studied.

Campfire ↔ Life

The edge containing Campfires and Life represents the interaction between information and application. This is the type of learning that takes place when you are working on a specific task and need more information to complete it. For example, if you are writing a document and need to create a table in your word processing program, you might refer to the manual (the Campfire) for information on table creation, and then immediately apply this information to the creation of a table in your document. In this situation there is no need for conversation unless the manual is so poorly written that you need to talk with an expert to learn how to do the task.

This pairing of learning spaces is well-suited to rapid clarification or gathering of background information once you are engaged in a contextual task.

Watering Hole ↔ Cave
The edge containing Watering Holes and Caves represents the interaction between conversation and reflection. This is the kind of learning that takes place when you have a meal with a colleague who shares some great ideas that drive the evening's conversation. You often experience the flow state during these events and, afterwards, need some quiet time to reflect on the concepts that were explored. These learning experiences can be incredibly rich and satisfying. They have even been the topic of movies such as *My Dinner with André*, the 1981 film directed by Louis Malle. In this film, two friends have dinner and the entire film is devoted to their conversation. You can be sure that the diners reflected on their conversation later that night.

I make it a point to eat lunch with interesting colleagues whenever I can. They function as my nutrient broth — a sounding board for my ideas, and a source of new thoughts that I then reflect on later when I am alone.

Watering Hole ↔ Life
The edge containing Watering Holes and Life represents the interaction between conversation and contextual application. Learning in this setting often centers around apprenticeship. Sometimes the process is quite informal. You can be working with a new program, for example, and need some help from someone nearby who has already mastered it. In the process of conversing with a peer around a topic germane to a specific task, the highly

contextual nature of the learning helps insure that it will be remembered.

Cave ↔ Life

The edge containing Caves and Life represents the interaction between reflection and application. This is the kind of learning we experience when we puzzle something out on our own. For example, I am not a big fan of technical manuals. As a result, when I get a new technical gadget to play with, I often try to figure out how to use it on my own without the benefit of reading a manual (the Campfire) or of talking with someone who already knows how the device works (the Watering Hole). If the process is successful, I feel justified in this process, but it often leads to frustration, especially if I'm working with something that I know very little about.

One goal of good user interfaces is to make something "intuitively" easy to use. Whenever someone talks about an intuitive user interface, they are implying that mere reflection in your Cave is all that will be needed to learn how to use the product. Directed instruction, if needed at all, is held to a minimum. While there are very few examples of intuitively easy devices or programs, there are legions of products that operate at the polar extreme — word processors whose manuals, for example, are larger than the documents you are trying to create. Much of the bloat that typifies today's software packages comes from the persistent belief that new features drive product sales, even if virtually none of the customers ever masters more than 15% of what the product is capable of doing. I am a fairly steady user of Adobe Photoshop, for example. This is the premiere graphics editing program on the market, and it is laden with features I've never used. Left to my own devices, I'd probably use less than 5% of Photoshop's capabilities. With the assistance of friends, manuals and magazine articles, I've expanded my skills to embrace about 10% of what this program has to offer.

If the Cave ↔ Life edge seems less useful than the others, this may be a telling commentary on the failure of designers to deliver on the "ease of use" promise.

As you can see, while each of these six edges of the tetrahedron plays a role in learning, none is sufficient in itself. Next we'll move from the edges to the four triangular faces of the tetrahedron. At this level we'll find some recognizable learning environments, and yet, even here, we'll find the picture to be incomplete.

The Faces (Triads)

Just-in-Case

Campfire, Watering Hole, Cave

This face is the home of informational, conversational and conceptual spaces. It lies opposite to the corner of Life, the contextual space. This face is home to "Just-in-Case" learning.

In some ways this face most resembles traditional school, at least in the early elementary grades where teachers spend less time lecturing and more time allowing students to converse and reflect. As children grow, traditional schools sacrifice Cave time first, and then start to replace conversational time with more lectures. By the time children enter college, the bulk of their courses are lecture-based, with conversational and reflective time being left to the students to find on their own.

From a pedagogical perspective, all three elements are needed. Harvard psychologist, Howard Gardner, for example, has developed a theory of multiple intelligences that was first introduced in his landmark book, *Frames of Mind*. In that book he proposed that each of us has components of seven distinct intelligences (now expanded to eight or nine) each of which can be employed in the service of learning. A current list of his intelligences includes:

- Linguistic
- Logical-Mathematical
- Intrapersonal
- Spatial
- Musical
- Bodily-Kinesthetic
- Interpersonal
- Taxonomic or Naturalist
  and,
- Existential

A traditional lecture and book-based classroom supports the first three on the list fairly well, but fails to meet the needs of students whose dominant intelligences fall among the remaining six.

As we'll explore later, modern telematic tools provide support for all the intelligences on this list. For now, let's see how Gardner's work might align to Campfires, Watering Holes and Caves.

The case can be made for applying each intelligence on Gardener's list in any environment: Campfire, Watering Hole, or Cave.

The Linguistic intelligence applies to language — clearly home to the Campfire, Watering Hole and Cave. The Logical Mathematical and Intrapersonal intelligences can be found in Caves, but also have their place in the other domains. The Musical, Bodily-Kinesthetic and

Interpersonal intelligences might have the Watering Hole as their primary home, while the Spatial, Taxonomic and Existential intelligences could be found anywhere in our triad.

As powerful as Gardner's work is, it lacks the direct connection to context. It is a theory of intelligence, not of application. This means that an educator could be doing a great job of honoring individual learning styles or strengths without any guarantee that what is learned will have an impact on students in their lives.

When students ask: "Why do I need to know this?" they are pleading for context. If the teacher answers: "Because it will be on a test," or, "Because you might need it later in life," (without being specific) this is a sign that context is missing and that the topic is being explored in a Just-in-Case manner.

As mentioned before, Just-in-Case learning happens when we are taught things "just in case" we will need them later without explaining just how this need might arise. The learning that takes place in this environment is decontextualized. It may, in fact, be highly relevant, but unless this relevance is demonstrated, the learner will be at a disadvantage. No one likes learning in the absence of meaning.

When I was in high school I had a wonderful experience in which a Just-in-Case requirement was made relevant (and paid off great dividends later). I wanted to take an advanced electronics course that was offered during the only period available for a required course in machining. I went to the head of the machine shop classes, asking for a waiver from his requirement since I had no plans to enter this field. In short, I'd just asked, "Why do I need this?" big time!

He looked up at me from his desk and said, "I'll tell you exactly why you need to take my course. I worked for over twenty years as a machinist, working day in and day out for people just like you. I know you, Thornburg; you are going to be an engineer someday. This means you'll be sitting in some nice air-conditioned office designing parts that people like me will be building for you. Unless you know how to use machine tools yourself, you'll design parts that are impossible to build, or that fail under the slightest stress, and all the blame will fall on the poor guys on the floor. There is no way I'm going to let you get out of this school without knowing how to build complex parts with your own two hands."

And so the matter was resolved, with me in his class instead of the one I had wanted to take.

The story picks up again years later when, with my freshly minted Ph.D., I showed up for work at the brand new Xerox Palo Alto Research Center (PARC). Like the other young scientists present, I had a long list of equipment to be built for my research. The backlog in the machine shop was months long, so I asked the head of the shop if I could be allowed to make my own equipment, using the machines during the workers' coffee breaks and lunch time. I still remember the crusty old machinist eyeing this greenhorn with disdain. He asked me to come back the next day.

When I returned he handed me a drawing for the most complex part I'd ever seen. "Make this and we'll talk," he said. I sweated blood making what, to my eyes, was the most beautiful piece of machining I'd ever seen. He took it from me, flipped down his magnifying lens, pulled out his micrometer and a deburring tool, and gave the part his measured gaze. After comparing the part against the drawing he asked, "Would you be happy with this piece of garbage?" I said I'd be thrilled with it (even if I was off by a few ten-thousands of an inch here and there). "Well," he said, "I guess there's no harm letting you work in here, but if you leave one scrap or fail to sharpen and return even one tool you will be banned forever, are we clear?"

I assured him I was very clear, and was able to gain a six-months advantage on my research because I had the requisite skills.

This incident illustrates that Just-in-Case learning can have its place when the context is explained.

Just-in-Time

Campfire, Life, Watering Hole
This face is the home of informational, contextual and conversational spaces. It lies opposite to the corner of the Cave, the conceptual or reflective space. This face is home to "Just-in-Time" learning.

Learning in fast-paced organizations often takes place using the spaces on this face. When you need to acquire a new skill, you may have time to attend a lecture or to seek the advice of a colleague, but your need to apply the skill to a pressing problem often cuts reflective time out of the picture.

There are some kinds of learning for which this is exactly the right approach, at least for the short term. Specifically, if you need instruction on a task with a short half-life to obsolescence, you might not need to reflect on the things you have learned. Anything that doesn't make sense will either get resolved through application or, if it doesn't, you can go back to the instructor or community of co-learners who helped you in the first place. It is uncommon in most businesses to see people engaged in reflective thought. The focus (at least in the fast-paced Silicon Valley culture I live in) is on application. This action-oriented approach to learning may have its place, but it also has its drawbacks. In the absence of reflection, there is pressure to find the "quick fix." In the computer software industry this has led to the creation of "bloatware," incredibly large applications whose size keeps growing as "improvements" are added incrementally, rather than by completely rethinking the product.

Another symptom of learning environments based on this face is the plethora of business books built around the quick-fix mantra. These books can be classified by brevity in time (The One-Minute Manager syndrome), or brevity in rules (The Seven Habits syndrome). The first business book author to create the "one-minute guide to seven effective principles" will become wealthy even if his or her customers never do find time to actually read the book. (Many years ago I wrote a small parody called *In Search of the One-Minute Megatrends* — a bold and astoundingly inept attempt to capitalize on the popular book themes of the day.)

While the realities of business life are fast-paced, the absence of reflective time can lead to disastrous consequences. The pressure to deliver on short notice can cause blindness to the long view. If every decision has to be right, risks are rarely taken, and this opens the door for new competitors.

Most high-tech companies are filled with employees who subscribe to a wide variety of magazines germane to their business. My sense is that the bulk of these magazines are either read at home, or are tossed into the trash after a cursory glance during lunch. The idea of a highly-educated professional spending hours of uninterrupted time in a research library is foreign to most fast-paced high-tech firms, no matter how valuable such time might be to the bottom line in the long term.

Just-in-Time learning has its place, but it is not a complete educational environment by itself.

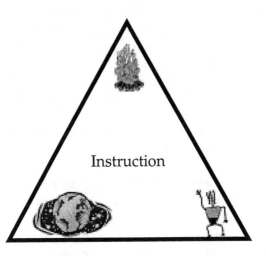

Instruction

Campfire, Cave, Life

This face is the home of informational, conceptual and contextual spaces. It lies opposite to the corner of the Watering Hole, the conversational space. This face is home to directed instruction.

In the extreme, this face describes the world of the secret societies in which information is passed on to initiates who are forbidden to share their emerging knowledge with anyone. The presentation of information in this world is highly structured, and information is presented only at certain times and in certain places. Francis Bacon said, "Knowledge is power." In his essay, *Empire*, he continues the theme: "And certain it is, that nothing destroyeth authority so much, as the unequal and untimely interchange of power pressed too far, and relaxed too much." What he meant was that, because power comes with knowledge, information should be shared judiciously (if at all) to insure the preservation of power in the hands of those who currently have it.

This face is home to concentrated power: a highly controlled autocratic environment where only a few people have a broad knowledge base, and the others are only given enough information to do their tasks. In traditional educational settings, this approach to learning applies to educators who are openly upset when students move ahead in a subject by themselves — especially if they acquire information about something the teachers don't know very much about.

In a corporate setting, this face is home to trade secrets: information that would be incredibly damaging if it ever left the company. Some corporations are so concerned about information theft that they make sure that employees are only given enough secret information to do their specific jobs, and that no one employee knows enough to reconstruct the secret information on his or her own.

As if to reinforce the absence of a Watering Hole in these environments, posters are often placed where people congregate (the water cooler, employee lounge, copying machine, or other natural conversational spaces) reminding people to not talk about company secrets. Phrases such as: "Loose lips sink ships" (popular during World War II) appear along with an image of zippered lips, just to be sure the message is clear.

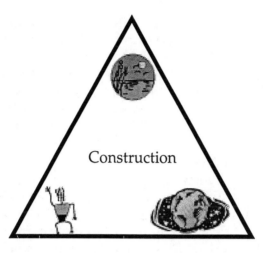

Construction

Watering Hole, Life, Cave

This face is the home of conversational, contextual and conceptual spaces. It lies opposite to the corner of the Campfire, the informational space. This face is home to the construction of knowledge.

The absence of a centralized source of information (the Campfire) creates a more free-wheeling atmosphere where people engage in creative dialog around the problems they are trying to solve. If the workgroup has sufficient diversity, the quality of the results can be spectacular, both in terms of the generation of novel solutions to problems, and in the timeliness of the results. Solutions based on "the way we always did this" are abandoned in favor of new ideas. This face functions quite well as home to creative problem solving when there are numerous ways to solve the problem. The Watering Hole becomes the place where people from diverse backgrounds can share their perspectives without fear of being trashed by a higher authority. This face is home to Kao's Law, named after the author John Kao who, in his excellent book, *Jamming*, said that creativity increases exponentially with the diversity and divergence of those connected to a network.

In traditional schools, special opportunities need to be created to foster this kind of problem-solving, since it is antithetical to the old structure based on information delivery.

In corporate settings the free-wheeling interchange of ideas among diverse groups of people from different departments is sufficiently rare that, when needed, special teams are assembled to work on a pressing problem. These teams are given tremendous autonomy, and they are often located in a separate building freed from the visual cues associated with their "normal" work environment. It is typical for such teams to have people from different backgrounds all working together — engineers, marketing people, manufacturing, sales, human resources, and people from other departments. This increases the likelihood of creative approaches to problem solving since there is no one dominant "expert" to take control of the problem-solving process.

People (students or workers) engaged in this type of activity experience real engagement with the subject. Competition, when it exists, comes without rivalry. People strive to do their best simply because it is enjoyable to be in the company of others who were (presumably) hand-picked to work on a pressing problem in a non-standard way. There is a deep sense of camaraderie and teamwork that emerges in this setting. No one is afraid of losing power by sharing ideas.

When Apple embarked on the project leading to the Macintosh, a diverse team of experts was settled into their own building. Based on a plan drafted by Jef Raskin, Steve Jobs set this group to work on the task of designing a new computer unencumbered by the architecture of the existing product. This dynamic team was working for the joy of finding the best solution to the challenge. They were secure in their knowledge and could share it without fear of losing power. The skull and crossbones pirate flag flew over their building at Apple, telling the world that they were charting their own course. The result was a computer that had almost nothing in common with the Apple II product line. It used a different microprocessor (the 68000 instead of the 6502), it had no user-accessible expansion slots (the Apple II had several), it used a new disk format and size (3.5" instead of 5.25"), and the user interface was designed to provide common elements across all applications so that users who knew how to save a file in a word processing program could use the same commands to save a file in a graphics program, for example. The Macintosh displayed documents as they would print (What you see is what you get).

When this new computer reached the market in 1984, every purchaser received the autographs of the Macintosh team — their signatures were etched inside the computer's housing.

It is hard to imagine how Apple could have moved forward into this new territory if the designers were \competing for funds and attention from the existing product teams. By abandoning everything from the past, including the operating system, Apple was able to create a smoothly running new architecture.

Contrast this with the evolution of Windows out of DOS. The Microsoft approach was completely different. While Apple was willing to abandon compatibility with previous software, Microsoft was not. This decision continues to haunt Microsoft, as anyone who has done a fresh install of Windows 95 can attest.

An effective "skunkworks" needs a clearly stated goal to be successful. This input comes at the start of the process, and its articulation sets the stage for the success (or failure) of the venture. While this initial statement has a Campfire quality to it, I tend to think of it less as a Campfire and more as the lighting of a fuse.

The Whole (Tetrahedron)

Face Pairings

You may have noticed that there is an interesting symmetry between face pairs: Campfire, Watering Hole and Cave (Just-in-Case) forms a resonating interval with Campfire, Life and Watering Hole (Just-in-Time). Similarly, Campfire, Cave and Life (Instruction) forms a resonating interval with Watering Hole, Life and Cave (Construction). The balance between these face pairings is natural, even though they each represent extremes.

These face pairings occur in various learning environments. For example, learners in the most abstract Just-in-Case learning environment still find numerous opportunities for Just-in-Time learning, even if they have to create these opportunities themselves. The more one face is accented, the more pressure there is for the other face to be applied. Learner demands for context become strongest when their instruction seems the least relevant. A wise educator will pay attention to the "Why do I need to know this?" question and adjust the teaching accordingly to bring the system into balance.

By the same token, a lecturer who sees the learners burning out from too much directed instruction will create opportunities for them to construct their own knowledge. In an ideal setting, the system will be self-correcting with the balance among the four faces coming from a natural give and take between the face pairings during the course of the learning experience.

To be complete, a learning environment requires a careful balance between all four corners and all four faces. Because of the balanced symmetry of the face pairings and of the corners to the opposing faces, it is as proper to say that a learning environment needs to have a balance of informational, conversational, conceptual, and contextual spaces, as it is to say it needs a balance between Just-in-Case, Just-in-Time, Instruction, and Construction.

In designing educational models based on these principles it is important to not fall into the trap of thinking that the four spaces need to be visited in sequence. Information does not necessarily precede conversation, nor does context always follow conceptualization. The flow between these spaces is highly dynamic — a swirling process in and among these spaces where each is visited, perhaps many times, during a course of study.

I saw an interesting example of this during a visit several years ago to Colégio Bandeirantes, a private high school in São Paulo, Brazil. Physics students were starting a unit on thermal expansion by conducting an experiment where the length of an aluminum rod was measured as it was heated. Students were able to see that the length of the rod increased with increasing temperature, without having been told in advance what to expect. They started in a contextual space of observing something in the real world. Next, they thought about what they had observed — they entered the Cave. This was followed by class discussion about the possible causes of this phenomenon (a

Watering Hole activity), and only then did the teacher fill in the gaps with the theoretical basis for thermal expansion. I was impressed by the efficacy of this approach, since it ran counter to the approach used by my teachers when I was in school. It was only many years later that I realized that this lesson worked because it balanced the four learning spaces.

From my perspective, Campfires, Watering Holes, Caves, and Life represent an educational framework that rekindles something from the past — primordial learning spaces that have existed as long as humans have learned. If the Web is to be an effective tool for learning, analogs of these spaces must either be found or invented. This is the major task of this book.

From Theory to Practice

The concept that all learning takes place in four spaces: Campfires, Watering Holes, Caves, and Life, is an interesting theory, but how does it fit in real classrooms? When I first started working on this concept I thought that Life (the contextual space) would be the weakest in our schools, and that the Campfire (informational space) would be the strongest, especially since the design of most classrooms facilitates lectures.

I am not alone in this belief. The cry for more context in education has been reaching a high pitch in the United States for many years. Bill Daggett, myself, and others, have lent their voice to the notion that content is not king — context is. The need for a balance of rigor *and* relevance is so great that, in 1994, the School-to-Work Opportunities Act was signed into law creating a Federal program to encourage states to create an educational system where each student was taught relevant information and skills needed for the careers of the coming century.

Relevance is welcome — like many, I remember asking my teachers why I needed to know what was being taught, with the reply: "Because it will be on the test." So, with this background in mind, I was interested in seeing how we were doing. How does Life measure up with the other three learning spaces in our classrooms?

In order to get a snapshot of actual classroom use of the learning spaces, I developed an inventory that explores teachers' assessment of their own use of these spaces, as well as their perception of the learning spaces honored in their classrooms and curriculum. (This inventory is available from the Thornburg Center.)

An early draft of the inventory was administered to about 100 educators attending a computer conference in the Spring of 1999. Self-administered assessments have their advantages and pitfalls. An advantage of self-administered assessments is that teachers know their own classrooms best, but there is a danger in that the person filling out the inventory might think he or she is spending a lot of time in a particular learning space, when, in fact, the bulk of the time is spent elsewhere. This error can be detected in part by having the inventory filled out by students and impartial observers as well as by the instructional staff. This was not done in our initial assessment, so the results might be skewed incorrectly; nonetheless, the results are interesting, as long as we accept them as reflecting the perceptions of the educators themselves.

The chart on the next page shows the relative strengths of the four learning spaces for our sample of 87 classroom teachers. The first four bars reflect the teachers' personal use of the learning spaces in their own lives, and the second set of four bars reflects their assessment of the reality of their classrooms.

84

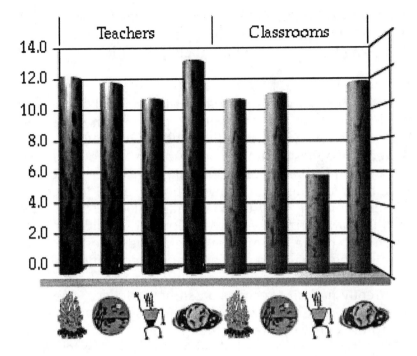

Starting with the teachers' set of four spaces, Life is the strongest, suggesting that the contextual space is dominant for educators. This result is not surprising given that teachers are always searching for new strategies they can apply with their students. The Campfire (informational space) came in a close second, yielding the Life-Campfire diad. This diad is characterized by the rapid application of information after it has been learned. The third highest score, the Watering Hole (conversational space), completes the definition of the dominant face of the tetrahedron: Campfires, Watering Holes, and Life — home to Just-in-Time learning. This result confirms many teachers' complaint that they rarely have time to reflect. Their days are dominated by the tyranny of the urgent, and time to reflect, look at the big picture, and develop their creativity is hard to find. Even so, the score for Cave time is not significantly different from the other learning space scores for the sample group of educators, suggesting that they have found ways to incorporate reflective/creative time into their schedules outside of school.

This all changes when we look at the second set of four bars reflecting the teachers' perception of their classrooms. As with the teachers themselves, Life (context) scored the highest, although not as highly in the classroom as in their personal lives. Our sample group of educators gave the Watering Hole (conversational space) the second highest score, yielding the Watering Hole-Life diad. This diad is characterized by conversation and application — a learning mode common to apprenticeship and cooperative learning. The increased emphasis of cooperative learning strategies in the past few decades has apparently had an effect on classroom practice. The third highest score, Campfire (informational space) once again completes the Just-in-Time learning face of the tetrahedron. The dominance of this face in the teachers' assessment of their classrooms is further established when we look at the score for the Cave (conceptual space). When viewed from the perspective of the classroom, the score for the Cave is about half that of the average for the other three spaces. This gap is statistically significant and reflects a huge challenge for education.

As mentioned in the previous chapter, the Cave is not only home to conceptual development, it is also home to much of our creative process. As creativity becomes a more important part of education (as I believe it will), it will be necessary to find ways to address the increased need for conceptual spaces in our schools.

The challenge of conceptual space is really the challenge of finding time for individual work on projects. Our schools are filled with so many things to do in a day that it becomes hard to find time where students can freely explore topics on their own. In-depth work often leads to the "flow" state described in the previous chapter. One of the dominant symptoms of flow is the loss of a sense of time — hours pass in minutes. It is hard to get engrossed in a project when bells go off every forty minutes or subjects are changed every hour.

The crisis of time has reached epidemic proportions in the United States, according to the 1994 report *Prisoners of Time*, published by the U.S. Department of Education (http://www.ed.gov). Unlike in most other developed nations, the amount of time spent in classrooms has remained the same for American schools over many years, even though numerous new demands have been placed on teachers' shoulders. Academic time has been stolen to make room for a host of non-academic activities; but the deepest flaw is the idea that learning can be doled out by the clock and defined by the calendar. Differences in individual learning rates are significant, yet our system makes no allowance for this. Given the pressure of our current school calendar, it is a wonder that students are given any time to reflect on what they are learning! Conceptual space (the Cave) is a casualty of this battle for time.

One approach to solving this problem is to have learners engage in conceptual tasks outside the classroom — after school. For some students this works, for others it does not. Too many learners have no quiet place where they can concentrate on a project and have access to the tools of creativity they need to cement their conceptual understanding. This opens the door to new opportunities to create after-school centers where people can have unlimited access to the tools they need to make up for the lack of adequate Cave time in school.

Once such spaces are found (either in or out of traditional schools), it is important that these places be equipped with adequate tools in support of the creative process and that they have an atmosphere that supports individual work without interruption.

Software that supports document creation ranging from text-based reports to interactive multimedia can play a critical role. It is also important that learners have access to Just-in-Time coaching on the effective use of these tools, or that we devote adequate time to letting students master these tools in the traditional educational setting.

It will be interesting to see how we address this need in the coming years.

Attributes of the Web

The previous chapters have dealt primarily with philosophies and theories of technology and education. My goal was to set the stage for our major task: identifying the intrinsic qualities of the Web as an educational tool. In order to do this, we need to leave the rear-view mirror behind and see the Web as a unique medium in its own right. Rather than explore what media the Web is most like, we'll focus on ways the Web is different from what has come before. I touched on this in an earlier chapter on hot and cool media. In this chapter we intensify the process.

The importance of this task can be seen from Henry Becker's recent study on Internet use by teachers (http://www.crito.uci.edu/TLC). Based on a survey of over 2,250 educators (4th through 12th grade) conducted in the Spring of 1998, he found that informational Web access represented the third largest use of technology in the classroom (after word processing and use of CD-ROM-based reference materials). This result is all the more significant when we take into consideration how few classrooms have meaningful high-speed access to the Internet. Becker's study shows that only 18% of the classrooms surveyed had high-speed access, and that 61%

of the classrooms had no access at all. As classroom access to the Internet increases, I would not be surprised to see the Web displace CD-ROM use for the number two spot within a year or two.

If we are going to be using the Web more and more in education at all levels (corporate education taking the lead in this regard), then it behooves us to know what makes the Web unique so we can use it to its greatest advantage. Failure to do this can hold us back. It reminds me of the story of the fellow who went to a store to return a chain saw. "You said this saw would let me cut wood in a fraction of the time it took me with my old hand saw, yet it ended up taking me five times as long. I want my money back!" The salesman looked at the saw to see if it was broken and, when it appeared to be in good shape, pulled the cord to start the gas engine. As soon as the engine started up the customer said, "Wow, what's that noise?" As long as we think of the Web as a library, a museum, a radio station, or any of the myriad things with which the Web has been compared, we are like the fellow who didn't know to start the engine of his chain saw. Tragically, much of what passes for "distance learning" on the Web has much in common with his story.

So, how is the Web unique?

1. *Communication is on-demand*
   Let's start by looking at the communication aspect of the Web. Most communication media are transient in that the information being passed from one location to the next is not saved. The telephone, radio and television are notable examples of this. We can choose to keep records of information conveyed to us through these media by the use of tape recorders, VCRs and the like, but the information itself is transient. In contrast, the

90

bulk of the information available on the Web resides on computers scattered all over the world so the same information can be accessed by multiple users at different times. The communication takes place between people and computers, not between people and other people (as with the telephone or live radio and television). The Web is an "on-demand" medium.

2. *The Web is an interactive medium*
In this regard the Web has something in common with the telephone. Both are interactive media in that nothing happens without the direct intervention of the users. This interactivity means that the "hotness" of push media (like radio or television) is replaced by the "coolness" of a pull medium in the case of the Web. To see this in action, let's look at radio. You can choose to listen to NPR when shows are broadcast (assuming there is a public broadcast radio station in your listening area), but, through the NPR web site (www.npr.org) you can listen to a previously broadcast program on a schedule of your own choosing, and can even listen to shows if there is no NPR affiliate broadcasting in your region.

3. *The Web supports multiple expressive modes*
The Web is a gateway to multiple expressive modalities (unlike TV, radio, newspapers, or books). Radio provides sound only — the images we associate with radio are created in our heads. You might, for example, have an impression of what a particular radio personality looks like, based on her speaking voice; and you might be surprised to see what this person really looks like if you encountered her in person. Because television provides the

viewer with sound and images, it removes that mystery from the our perception.

Both radio and television are linear sequential media that push with such force that reflection is precluded. If you want to pause a broadcast to think about what you just heard or saw, this option is closed to you with traditional broadcast media. Print-based media are different in this regard. You can pause while reading this book, for example, to think about what you've just read. You can, if you choose, mark a passage for further reflection at a later time. The static permanent nature of print is an advantage in this regard, yet it does not allow the dynamic representation of information provided by television or (to a lesser extent) radio.

The Web brings the dynamism of broadcast media and the reflective capability of text together in a unique way. This is not just a merger of media types, but something new. Text can be marked or copied for later reference, but so can sounds and animations. The on-demand nature of the Web (mentioned in the previous section) allows us to treat all media types with the same flexibility we associate with any of the separate media types by themselves. This gives the Web the capacity to be used for learning in ways that are, thus far, largely untapped.

4. *The Web supports representational choice*
Because of the Web's support for multiple media types, it provides the opportunity for true representational choice. For example, many informational Web sites give users the option to see "text-only" versions of a page, usually to eliminate the long download time associated with pages with

lots of graphics. While this option is provided as a feature for users with slow modems, it could be expanded to embrace individual preferences for information retrieval and presentation. For example, sites rich with numerical data can (in principle) be designed to allow users to see the data in a variety of ways: as tables of numbers, as graphs of various kinds, as animated images reflecting the changes in data over time, and even as sounds or melodies. Furthermore, the user could choose which form to have the data presented and change the presentation mode at any time.

This capability is intrinsic to the Web (especially with the increased use of Java), but few attempts have been made to offer this flexibility to users. My guess is that failure to embrace this capability of the Web comes from a continued reliance on the rearview mirror. As long as we think of the Web as a radio station, or a newspaper, etc., thoughts of supporting multiple expressive modalities would never arise. A more effective message for the Web comes from the fast-food provider who offers to "make it your way." A carefully designed Web site could (in principle) let you get information in the way that is most natural to you.

5. *The Web is a non-conserved medium*
Of all the metaphors used to describe the Web, the concept of the Web as library is among the most dominant. The "good news, bad news" joke says: The Web is the world's largest library (good news), but the bad news is that all the books are piled on the floor. There is much to be said in support of the library as a metaphor for the Web. Skills of librarianship are tremendously important to

anyone trying to find information on the Web, although even here the library metaphor holds us back. Most search engines, for example, support Boolean searching which, while effective for moderately small static collections of documents found in physical libraries, can prove to be unwieldy and unsatisfactory when searching the 400 million or so publicly accessible Web pages whose number grows second by second.

But the greatest challenge to the library metaphor deals with another aspect of the "size" of the Web's collection: only one copy is needed for each document. In physical libraries, a book can be checked out by one reader at a time, unless the library has purchased multiple copies. Physical libraries have to trade off breadth for depth. This is especially apparent for the "libraries" from which we rent videotapes. Tape rental agencies have to decide how many copies to get of each new film to be sure that they don't alienate their customers by running out of copies. Yet, a few week after release, the demand for a tape drops sharply, and the tape rental shop is stuck with inventory that is no longer generating revenue.

The Web stands in sharp contrast to this situation. Every time you look at a document on the Web, you have caused the Web to publish a copy of this document on your computer. This frees up the Web server to handle other users while you are perusing the page you requested. These copies are stored in a special place on your hard drive and are removed when that storage space is needed for other documents. This process is important. Instead of "looking" at a document, you are first making a copy of it and looking at the copy. (There are a few exceptions to this, but generally every document you see on your screen is stored on your computer first.) If a physical library operated this way, you'd find the book you wanted, make a copy of it, and then take the copy home and throw it out two weeks later when it was "due." This would be tremendously wasteful in the physical world, but is tremendously efficient in the world of bits. Bandwidth is still a scarce resource, so anything that moves Web use "off-line" is worth doing.

An important consequence of this unique property of the Web is that a single posting of a document can be obtained by any of the millions of Web users who are able to gain access to the site. When the Sojourner robot started exploring Mars, millions of people downloaded the first images taken from the surface of this planet, completely swamping the computers at NASA and their mirror sites. In the face of such demand, the original images at NASA were copied to other sites (the mirrors) to handle the overload. Even so, it took only a dozen or so "originals" to serve millions of requests. This level of service is trivial in the world of bits, but is inconceivable in the world of atoms.

Physical artifacts are conserved media: if I give you a book, I no longer have it. Web artifacts are not conserved: copies of documents are published on your computer on demand.

6   *Barriers to publishing are low*
Virtually anyone with access to the Web has the capacity to create and publish a Web site. Almost all Internet service providers provide some space on their servers for use by their customers, and millions of personal Web sites have emerged as a result.

Free Web-page creation tools are available to allow just about anyone with a little computer experience to create Web pages complete with text, tables, graphics, and all the other representational modes for information you can think of. The result of freely available authoring tools and server space is such that almost any Web user can become a Web publisher.

This aspect of the Web represents a sharp break from the current model of publishing and represents a retrieval (in part) of aspects of the scribal manuscript culture. Prior to the invention of the mass-produced book, authorship resulted in a single manuscript that was shared with a close circle of readers, some of whom might have the manuscript copied for their own library. The idea of creating copies in advance of having identified readers for each copy was foreign to the manuscript culture — books were far too expensive to reproduce unless you already had a customer in place.

All this changed with the development of mass-produced books. Once the type was set, the incremental cost of additional copies was quite low. This allowed the creation of "publishers" as distinct entities. Authors now interacted with publishers, not with their readers directly. The publisher took on several roles, including proof-reading, editing, typesetting, printing, warehousing, marketing, and distributing the books. The publisher took on another role as well: gate keeping. In order for a book to be published, the publisher needed to be convinced there was a sufficiently large audience to cover the costs of bringing the finished volume to market. This placed tremendous power in the hands of editors who developed their own criteria for deciding whether or not a book should be published. While this provided a service to potential readers who knew that someone thought enough of the book to see it through to the marketplace, it also closed the door to authors whose ideas were not seen as commercially viable. Almost every successful author has tales of rejection letters sent from publishers whose editors failed to see the merit of their work in the early years. Of course, this pendulum swings both ways. Once an author is successful, the barrier to publication evaporates and new offerings from this author are welcomed, even if their merit is questionable. Fame implies authority, as seen in the books published within weeks of a tawdry trial by jurors or others who claim some "inside knowledge."

The Web breaks the hold of the publisher, rekindling the direct connection between reader and author that marked the scribal era. Unlike that era, however, the Web affords access to a huge audience. While I have, for example, posted short articles on my Web site for my friends to see, they are there for the public at large, if they are so inclined to view them. The barriers to publishing have evaporated. As with many aspects of new media, this is a mixed blessing. Gone is the "vetting" of editors, the accuracy checks of proof-readers, and the layout of professional designers. In its place is the sharing of raw ideas, some of which may be of tremendous value and are expressed in a pleasing way. The sheer volume of self-published material on the Web staggers the imagination and has incurred the wrath of those who claim we are drowning in "infoglut." But, when viewed from another perspective, the Web's low barrier to

97

publishing can be seen as a liberating influence for creativity. New poems, works of art, videos, musical compositions, and other expressions find ample room to co-exist on the Web. And, just as millions can share their ideas, millions can experience them as well. The death of gate keeping may result in the Web being the driving force for a creative upsurge that makes the Renaissance pale in comparison.

What's next?

There are more unique characteristics of the Web waiting to be discovered; the unique nature of the Web comes into view slowly, like a photograph being developed. The six attributes presented above are but a starting point to break the connections with the media of the past.

OK, but so what? Suppose you are designing a distance learning course using the Web. How do these six qualities of the Web affect your design methodology?

One way to structure the design is to operate on the assumption that the Web will be used primarily to do things that can't be done more effectively with other media. This is a challenge for educational technology use in general. There are still some schools that have students use expensive computer systems for decontextualized drill and practice that can be done with far less expensive resources (such as paper workbooks). Until networked computers are in the palms and backpacks of every student, we should be sure that these resources are used in the most effective and unique manner possible.

So, in designing a Web-based course, we might start by asking the following questions:

1. *How do course materials take advantage of the fact that Web-based communication is on-demand?*
   Does the course design allow users to interact with materials anywhere, anytime?

2. *How does the course incorporate interactivity?*
   Does the course take advantage of learners' active involvement with the materials instead of just presenting information to be read or watched on the screen?

3. *How does the course support multiple expressive modes?*
   Does the course take advantage of text, sound, video, interactive simulations in the process of engaging the leaner with the content?

4. *How does the course support representational choice?*
   Are learners encouraged to explore information in representational modes natural to them as opposed to restricting information to a pre-defined mode chosen by the course authors?

5. *How does the course support the wide distribution of information?*
   Are course materials available for download so they can be explored off-line as appropriate? Does the course design support the free interchange of documents among learners?

6. *How does the course support publication of learner's work?*
   Does the course build in the capability for learners to post their own work to the Web for use as a resource by other learners?

These are just some questions that can be asked when designing instructional materials for the Web. But, as we have seen in previous chapters, we also need to insure that, as with any educational environment, Web-based instruction incorporates elements of all four learning spaces: Campfires, Watering Holes, Caves and Life. The following chapters address this topic.

Campfires, Watering Holes, Caves, and Life on the Web

At long last we have come to the chapter that addresses the use of the Web in education. As you might guess, our focus will be on the four learning spaces and their analogs in the on-line world. If (as proposed in earlier chapters) learning requires four spaces, then for on-line learning to be effective it must mirror these spaces as well. This does not mean, however, that the Web has to replicate other media to accomplish this task. For example, while a lecture can be delivered through Web-based video playback, there are other ways (some of them unique and more powerful) through which the Web can present information to learners. In the remainder of this chapter, we'll explore Campfires, Watering Holes, Caves and Life as supported by the Web and other Internet-based tools. Some of our examples will replicate other media (such as radio) and some will not. In embracing the new, it is not always necessary to throw out the old.

This chapter is, by no means, meant to provide a comprehensive list of sites and tools for learning — such a list is impossible to create with the Web doubling in size every few months. Instead we'll show some examples that make our point, and that might be interesting to a general audience. The examples draw largely from traditional (as opposed to corporate) learning environments just because most interesting corporate learning sites are hidden behind firewalls, blocking access to most readers of this book.

As this book is being written, the Web is primarily accessed through programs called "browsers," of which Netscape and Microsoft are the major producers. In addition to providing access to Web pages, full-featured browsers (such as Netscape Communicator and Microsoft's Internet Explorer) provide the capacity to view Web pages (HTML documents), as well as newsgroups and e-mail — other services provided over the Internet. The Web pages displayed in the latest browsers can be quite complex, supporting text, images, simple animation and sophisticated programs built in Javascript or Java. Through the addition of "plug-ins," additional media types can be supported, including audio, video, and a host of special document formats. The extensibility of browser capabilities through the use of these plug-ins insures that the Web can constantly evolve to accommodate new media types as they are developed. This flexibility, commonplace to the Web today, is rarely found in any other type of software. It represents one of the Web's greatest strongholds for long-term viability as a learning tool.

As powerful as browsers are, they represent only one of the kinds of tools used to access information delivered over the Internet. Other tools allow the navigation and exploration of media types for which the traditional HTML-based document is not appropriate. Sometimes this information can be accommodated through a browser plug-in, but often this is not the best choice, so specialized software needs to be used. Even in these cases, though, developers work very hard to provide as seamless an interface as possible to the user's workhorse — the browser program — which is often open in another window at the same time the specialized software is being used.

It is safe to say that the Web has migrated a long way from its origins as a tool for the display of hypertext documents. Today's rich multimedia browsers handle text documents as well (if not better) than the first text-only programs, yet have evolved in ways limited only by the imagination and creativity of the programmers creating tools for this medium. This continued burst of creative energy will help the Web become an even more powerful tool for learning than it is today.

Campfires

The Campfire is the informational learning space — the space the Web was originally intended to occupy. In the physical world of learning, this space is populated by traditional information delivery methods: lectures, books, audio programming, videotapes, instructional television, and so on. In this world information is often hard to find. Physical libraries are expensive to maintain, and collection size is limited to a tiny fraction of publicly available printed information. Experts are physically isolated from most learners, and teachers typically reach fewer than a hundred learners at a time. In the physical world, Campfire-based teaching treats information as a scarce resource. Teachers focus on providing information to learners in a highly structured manner so they acquire the foundational knowledge they need to thrive in life.

In fact it is not the information that is scarce in the real world, only meaningful access to it. As Mark Nelson states in a 1994 article entitled *We Have the Information You*

Want, But Getting It Will Cost You: Being Held Hostage by Information Overload (emphasis is from the original):

> Consider that more new information has been produced within the last three decades, than in the last **five millennia.** Over 9,000 periodicals are published in the United States each year, and almost 1,000 books are published daily around the world. The November 13, 1987, issue of *The New York Times* numbered 1,612 pages, containing about 2,030,000 lines and over **twelve million** words.

While "infoglut" has become a popular term today, note that the size reference for *The New York Times* is taken from an issue published in 1987 — almost half a decade before the Web was launched. If we feel swamped by information today, it is not merely because there is so much of it, but that our access to this information has dramatically increased. The major impact of the Web as an informational tool has nothing to do with the volume of information, it comes from the *access* it provides to information. When libraries are built from bits instead of atoms, huge informational repositories can reside on modest disk drives scattered throughout the world. The complete works of Shakespeare occupy a volume of several hundred pages, weighing about a kilogram, yet the text from these works fits easily on four floppy disks.

There are literally hundreds of millions of publicly accessible informational Web sites competing for our attention. Unlike students confined to a classroom, Web-based learners are a single mouse click away from leaving for another on-line destination. This freedom to move provides additional reasons for wanting to insure that the information learners are getting is accurate, relevant, and presented in a way that supports individual learning styles. Students who would never dare walk out of a boring lecture will drop out of a boring Web site in a heartbeat. Effective informational Web sites need to communicate their content clearly and need to keep their users engaged. While the situation changes slightly for captive sites whose use is required by an on-line course, even these sites often provide links to more general destinations on the Web, from which users can click their way to oblivion.

Web-based Campfires have another characteristic that distinguishes them from lectures, audio and video programming: time on task is determined by the learner, not by the educator. A lecture may have a 50 minute duration, constrained by class schedules. A visit to an informational Web site might last a few minutes or many hours, based on many factors including available time, the engagement of the learner, and the depth of relevant content. In this regard the informational Web is similar to a book in its capacity to engage people and carry them into a state of flow where time seems to evaporate. This aspect of informational Web sites presents a tremendous challenge to the use of the Web in traditional schools. The idea of fixed class periods is at odds with the way we use the Web.

As school-based educators explore the Web as one of their sources of content, they need to keep these issues in focus. The sheer volume of high-quality information available for free on the Web is, by any account, staggering. It is hard to imagine any subject for which relevant Web sites could not be found. Even so, some educators find the Web more useful than others. Henry Becker's 1999 study, *Internet Use by Teachers*, found that, among high school teachers, math educators' level of perceived value in the Web was about half that of all other teachers. This result is perplexing given the large number of informational Web sites devoted to the exploration of mathematical topics of all kinds. But it does illustrate that adoption of the Web into education varies widely, even as it is increasing overall.

Informational Web sites of value to education are abundant. One source, devoted exclusively to material provided by public sources (Library of Congress, Smithsonian Institution, etc.) is the FREE directory hosted by the U. S. Department of Education (http://www.ed.gov/free) as a result of a 1997 Presidential order to all federal agencies instructing them to determine what resources they could make available to enrich the Web as a tool for teaching and learning. This site is organized by subject area (art, language, mathematics, social studies, etc.) and provides links to hundreds of sites containing material of high quality. In addition to providing links to information, supporting agencies are looking for educators with whom they can partner to gear their collections to defined educational goals.

Another rich source of links to quality information in numerous subject areas is the GEM Project (Gateway to Educational Materials, http://www.thegateway.org). As of May 25, 1999, the Gateway contained over 6,600 educational resources distributed among seventeen categories ranging from Art to Vocational Education. Within each category, further divisions are provided. Math, for example, is divided into twenty-two subtopics covering just about every aspect of math education in the K-12 curriculum.

FREE and GEM are two excellent resources for those who want high-quality material that has been evaluated for relevance and accuracy. Because almost all the material comes from public or non-profit sources, users are not bombarded with advertising or commercial points of view sometimes found at other sites.

The Web's capacity to present information in many formats gives a further advantage to some of these sites. Unlike textbooks, they are generally free or inexpensive, timely, and (in many cases) they provide information in forms for which there is no printed counterpart. To give one extreme example, (although it uses a special viewer instead of your Web browser), a program called Planet Earth (available as shareware from http://www.download. com) provides a view of our planet that is updated from the Internet to show the current cloud cover. The globe can be rotated and the user can zoom in for a closer look at a particular area. Major cities are shown as dots and, when the mouse is moved near a city, its name and local time appears on the screen. Cloud images are provided by the University of Wisconsin-Madison Space Science and Engineering Center (http://www.ssec.wisc.edu). This application performs a task that is virtually impossible to provide any other way.

This program can be used by anyone with a casual interest in weather patterns, or it can become a tool for those who want to study meteorology in more depth.

Planet Earth

The number of excellent informational Web sites is enormous. Two examples that leap to mind are the Library of Congress American Memory Project (http://memory.loc.gov) and the rich collection of Web sites associated with NASA and its various projects (http://www.nasa.gov). As with many other sites, these make in-depth information that was once restricted to a few select people available to everyone.

Access to the physical collection of the Library of Congress is limited to those over the age of 18 who are in physical proximity to the library. If you want to examine a rare document, access is further limited to researchers who need to be able to see a document that is fragile, sensitive to light, or irreplaceable. If you've even visited the rare book room of a library, you already know the kinds of hurdles that are placed in your way. You often need to wear special gloves and a face mask. The room is very dimly lit, and you are not allowed to bring a pen into the room. You are also (generally) not left alone when you are there.

The American Memory project at the Library of Congress eliminates all these problems. It provides access to rare documents by digitizing them and making high-resolution images of these documents available at their Web site for all to see and use.

Let's say you are interested in exploring the history of Bell's invention of the telephone. In the past you might have read several books on the topic, some of which quote from Bell's correspondence and notes. Now, anyone with access to the Web can examine his letters and lab notes directly. Digitized images of his material are accompanied by transcripts of their content (for those who have a hard time reading Bell's handwriting). The sense of connection with the history of the telephone gained by access to images of the actual source material is far greater than what one gets by reading a book on the topic. (Bell's letters and other documents can be found at http://memory.loc.gov/ammem/bellhtml/bellhome.html.)

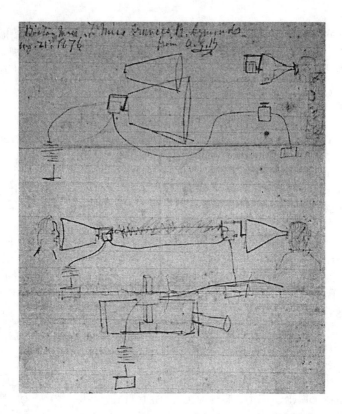

In addition to providing unlimited universal access to rare paper-based documents, the Library of Congress uses the Web to bring other media to a wider audience as well. For example, a sub-site, *Inventing Entertainment: The Motion Pictures and Sound Recordings of the Edison Companies* (http://memory.loc.gov/ammem/edhtml/edhome.html) traces the history of Thomas Edison and the recording and film companies he created. This site contains 341 films and hundreds of sound recordings that can be played through the browser. Rare recordings, such as Zez Confrey's 1921 recording of his famous ragtime piece, *Kitten on the Keys*, can be downloaded for later playback, or can be listened to in real-time. The incorporation of multiple media types, any of which can be accessed with a simple click of the mouse, represents one of the unique qualities of the Web as an informational medium. No other communication medium provides the flexibility to immediately move from text to images, to sounds, to movies. The Library of Congress uses the Web quite effectively in this regard.

Moving from history to events on the current horizon, NASA's suite of Web sites also makes effective use of the unique properties of the Web. As with the Library of Congress, NASA makes available to all what was once only available to a few. New discoveries and logs of ongoing projects share space with descriptions of future missions.

The starting point for NASA's presence on the Web, (http://www.nasa.gov), is a natural place to find information on all NASA-related activities, past, present and future. As with the Library of Congress, NASA provides support for the presentation of information in a variety of media formats. For example, those interested in the International Space Station can see a map of the globe on which the space station's location is continuously updated, along with detailed information on its speed, altitude, and exact location.

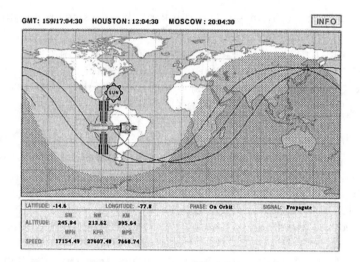

Spacelink (http://spacelink.nasa.gov), a special site for educators and learners, provides access to materials connected to various curricular areas, and even provides access to specific curriculum support through a special sub-site (http://spacelink.nasa.gov/Instructional.Materials/Curriculum.Support).   Other educational support is provided through more specialized sites (e.g., http://education.nasa.gov and http://learn.ivv.nasa.gov), making NASA a major provider of quality information on all aspects of planetary and space science.

NASA also helps host special projects for students, such as the Mars Millennium 2030 project (http://www.mars2030.net) — a project in which students design communities for habitation on Mars in the year 2030.   This project has several sponsors, including NASA, National Endowment for the Arts, the U. S. Department of Education, The J. Paul Getty Trust, The White House Millennium Council, and Jet Propulsion Laboratories. This project (starting in the Fall of 1999) blends science with the arts in a way that provides maximum flexibility for children's projects in almost any grade level. While this project formally ends in mid-2000, its framework can be used for creative projects conducted any time.

NASA and the Library of Congress are providers of rich educational material, but their content is not geared around specific courses of study. One corporate Web site that provides more structure in this regard is the Sunergy site operated by Sun Microsystems (http://www.sun.com/sunergy). Sunergy is a multi-faceted, interactive, educational program from Sun Microsystems that addresses current information technology (IT) issues. The program uses a mix of media and technology to exchange information with a worldwide audience. Each program focuses on one aspect of information technology and its impact on society or business. The emphasis, of course, is directed to Sun's corporate vision, but this is to be expected. Sunergy programs are broadcast as videos through satellite transmissions, but they can also be explored (both as videos and as written transcripts) at the Web site. The Web site also provides in-depth reference and background material when appropriate, extending the value of the programs.

Sun has taken a leadership role in making some of its professional development material available to the general public at no charge. Presumably these programs help potential Sun employees acquire the skills they need to work in this industry. In any event, it would be great to see more high-tech firms who are willing to bring some of their non-proprietary staff development courses to a wider audience, especially since there is a tremendous shortage of qualified applicants for jobs in most high-tech industries.

While many informational Web sites have done an excellent job of incorporating several media types, few have yet provided their users with the flexibility to retrieve information in different ways. One site that has made significant strides in this direction is the World Data Interactive site (http://www.wdatai.com). Subscribers to this site can gain access to databases provided by agencies all over the world and can then create graphs using tools of their own, or, using World Data's Discovery graphing package, can look for correlation between data (e.g., GNP and arable land). Data sets for this site come from numerous sources: U. S. Department of Commerce, United Nations, Center for Disease Control, etc. All of the data from these sources is provided in a consistent format (tab-delimited plain text) so it can be used with a variety of programs for display and analysis. The user is free to choose how the data is presented. Data can be viewed in numerical form, or as graphs. Graphs can show multiple data sets over time or can plot one data set against another.

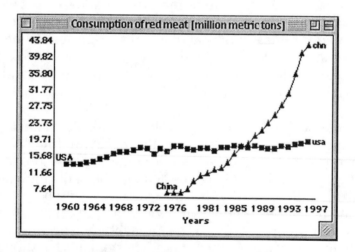

Future development in informational Web sites will probably include greater flexibility for the user in determining how information is to be presented. This shift is bringing the Web into its own as a medium of expression, and providing Campfire experiences that are impossible to achieve with other tools of communication.

114

Watering Holes

The Watering Hole is the conversational learning space — the space where peers interact. In the physical world of learning, this space is populated by classroom discussions, conversations at coffee houses, or informal conversations around the water cooler or copying machine. In this world information sharing is often spontaneous and unstructured. While it is often intentional (especially in a classroom setting), chance encounters between peers also provide powerful opportunities to share information.

The bulk of physical world interaction is synchronous. Conversations over the telephone or face to face are far more commonplace than extended dialogs that take place through the exchange of letters. In the world of the Internet, on the other hand, asynchronous communication (e-mail) is more commonplace than real-time chat. This is probably because e-mail is so easy to create and send. When you get an e-mail from someone, you can read it and respond immediately. Your return message is usually delivered right away, allowing several exchanges of information to take place in a short period of time. This stands in stark contrast to physical mail where, at best, it takes a day for a message to reach its recipient. As the time-lag between sending and receiving messages increases, there is a greater tendency for the messages to be informational rather than conversational in tone.

On-line Watering Holes fall into two broad categories: asynchronous and synchronous. While some of the tools in each category use the Web, some preceded the Web by many years. In fact, the history of the Internet reflects a balance between information and conversation dating back to its origins.

According to *Hobbes' Internet Timeline* (http://www.isoc.org/guest/zakon/Internet/History/HIT.html), a functional e-mail system was running on computer networks as early as 1972. This system, developed by Ray Tomlinson at the consulting firm Bolt, Beranek, and Newman, introduced the use of the "@" sign in e-mail addresses. When the Internet was created the following year, specifications for file transfer were established, assuring that the Internet functioned both for asynchronous communication (e-mail) and information delivery (file transfer). While rudimentary real-time chat systems were developed in the early years, the Internet Relay Chat (IRC) system was developed much later, in 1988, by Jarkko Oikarinen. By the time Tim Berners-Lee introduced the world to the Web in 1991, the foundations for information delivery and communication were already well in place. The release of Mosaic from the University of Illinois in 1993 gave the Web its graphical user interface, and provided much of the look and feel we still encounter when exploring the Net. It is important to understand that the goal of the Web was not to replace other Internet technologies, but to incorporate and extend them through (initially) the use of hypertext, and then through the use of a graphical user interface.

Most people create and read e-mail with special software designed for the purpose, such as Eudora, (http://www.eudora.com). Most full-featured Web browsers have built-in support for e-mail. There is another option, however, that is gaining in popularity: the use of Web-based e-mail systems such as Hotmail (http://www.hotmail. com) and similar services. If you want to check your home e-mail account from the Web, you can do this through a service called Mailstart Plus (http://www.mailstartplus.com), or (for AOL users) at http://netmail.web.aol.com. The advantage of Web-based mail systems is that they can be accessed anywhere you have access to the Internet. When I am out of the United States, I rely on Web-based e-mail because I can log on to my account from any computer connected to the Internet. While most Web-based e-mail services do not support the rich variety of attachments that can be accommodated with traditional e-mail tools, the benefit of having access from any connected computer anywhere on the planet makes this service quite valuable. My guess is that, soon, Web-based e-mail will offer all the features associated with current dedicated e-mail systems.

As for the future of e-mail, the opportunities are tremendous. For example, many e-mail programs already support parts of HTML, allowing messages to acquire the look of Web pages, complete with links. Continued work in this domain will probably lead to e-mail with images, selection buttons, and other features. Taken to the extreme, the only future difference between e-mail and the Web may be that one of them is a "push" medium (e-mail) and the other is a "pull" medium.

Of course, one advantage of purely text-based e-mail is that messages can be downloaded quickly even over low-speed connections. This was important years ago, but is becoming much less of an issue today. In the 1970s I had access to the Net using a 300 b/sec modem — and I thought that was fast. According to a study conducted by Colleen Kehoe and her colleagues at Georgia Tech (*GVU 10th WWW User Survey*, http://www.gvu.gatech.edu/user_surveys/survey-1998-10), as of November, 1998, only 1.8% of Web users were connecting through 14 kb/sec modems or slower. Users operating between 28 and 56 kb/sec accounted for 64.5% of all users. Today inexpensive broadband services are expanding their reach into homes and businesses of all sizes. Telephone companies are promoting ADSL, a service that allows Net download speeds in excess of one million bits per second, and cable operators are offering services such as @Home, operating at speeds up to three million bits per second. The GVU study showed that 27.5% of users were gaining access to the Web at megabit or faster speeds. It is clear that users take advantage of speed increases as quickly as possible. As broadband services become universal, barriers to the transformation of e-mail from pure text to richly formatted documents will evaporate.

E-mail is the most popular asynchronous communication tool, but it is by no means the only one. Other popular tools include newsgroups and listservs. Newsgroups are like bulletin boards devoted to specific topics. Someone who posts a message to a newsgroup can have their message read by anyone who wants to browse the group. As with most e-mail, newsgroups are not Web-based (yet). They are so popular, though, that full-featured Web browsers provide support for newsgroups.

The sheer volume of newsgroups is staggering. As of June, 1999, my service provider hosted about 29,000 newsgroups. Newsgroup topics span the range of human interests. Groups like alt.music-lover.audiophile.hardware or alt.tv.ally-mcbeal will appeal to certain individuals. Hobbyists can access over sixty groups on collecting. Math enthusiasts have over seventy groups from which to choose, and history buffs will find seventy-five or so newsgroups just for them. There are about 112 newsgroups devoted to various aspects of education. Windows aficionados and foes alike will find much of interest in the 270 different newsgroups devoted to this operating system.

In addition to the vast number of these groups, many of them contain thousands of postings. To make matters more challenging, the "signal to noise" ratio for many newsgroups is quite low. Because virtually anyone can post something to a group, messages of great relevance and accuracy appear along with irrelevant information and diatribes. Effective newsgroup participants have to develop skills to separate the wheat from the chaff.

Listservs operate like newsgroups, but send their postings directly to your e-mail address. Instead of having to make a special visit to your favorite newsgroups, listservs update you with each new posting as it is received. The number and scope of listservs rivals that of newsgroups, although they represent two different approaches to asynchronous communication. One place to locate listservs is at http://tile.net/lists. This site lets you search for lists by topic, and is a great starting place for anyone interested in this form of communication. As with newsgroups, the number of available lists is huge — in the thousands. The number of lists relating to three topics mentioned above (education, math and history) are similar to those we found for newsgroups.

Both newsgroups and listservs can be moderated or unmoderated. Moderated lists are generally of higher quality because incoming messages are not posted until they have been reviewed by the list's moderator. While this helps keep the list on track, it can also result in the censorship of valuable opinions. Unmoderated lists, on the other hand, pass on every message they receive. This can lead to stimulating exchanges of opinions, or degenerate into meaningless drivel. For this reason, you should subscribe to newsgroups and listservs judiciously, and unsubscribe from those that fail to meet your needs as soon as possible to avoid information overload.

Web-based conferencing is yet another asynchronous communication medium that is gaining in popularity. Unlike e-mail and listservs which push their content to the user, Web-based conferencing requires that the participant visit a special Web site to take part in a conference. This presents special challenges as David Woolley says in *The Future of Web Conferencing* (http://thinkofit.com/webcon/wcfuture.htm):

> The biggest challenge facing most Web conferencing sites is simply getting people to visit regularly. Enticing people to take a look at a Web site is one thing; getting them to make a habit of returning every day is much more difficult. It takes effort to visit a site to see if there is anything new, and the activity there must consistently be useful and compelling, or most people will fall out of the habit of checking in. Some people never form the habit even if the content is useful, simply because there is nothing to remind them to check the conference.
>
> Discussions that take place over e-mail lists don't have this problem. E-mail discussions come to you, rather than you having to go look for them.
>
> Whereas it requires continuing regular effort to check a Web conference, it requires effort to stop receiving messages from an e-mail list. Once you have subscribed to a list, you must take conscious action in order to unsubscribe.
>
> For this reason alone, e-mail lists have a natural tendency to accumulate participants over time, while Web conferences have a natural tendency to lose participants.

Because Web-based conferencing takes place inside existing Web pages, it provides a potential to blend Campfires and Watering Holes in a very effective manner. For example, an ongoing conference on the evolving role of technology in education is maintained by the Academy for Educational Development through their Millennium Project (http://millennium.aed.org). This project maintains separate conferences on different topics relating to the impact of technology on education. Each of these topics is introduced through an essay by an expert who sets the stage for the dialog. Experts tapped for these conferences include leaders in the field — people like Frank Withrow, Kathleen Fulton, Chris Dede, and others who are well-known and articulate spokespeople for their positions. In addition to brief essays from experts, visitors to the site are provided with bibliographies of relevant materials, both on- and off-line. A conference on a particular subject can be joined by anyone with an idea to share. Popular topics generate numerous responses, and the Web conferencing software (WebBBS, a shareware cgi script from http://awsd.com/scripts/webbbs) automatically maintains the "threads" of the discussion. A thread is a series of messages that respond to a single message, or to previous responses to this message. This feature makes it easy for visitors to keep up with subsets of the conference of greatest interest to them.

As mentioned by David Woolley, the big challenge of Web-based conferencing is getting people to visit regularly. It helps when the conferences deal with engaging topics and are led by recognized experts, but even these conferences fail to generate nearly the enthusiasm of the dialog found in an active listserv or newsgroup.

Once again, as bandwidth increases, the time needed to access Web-based conference sites will cease to be an issue. The fact that conferences take place in the context of informational Web pages brings tremendous value to this mode of interaction, especially in a learning environment. The future for Web-based conferencing looks bright.

While asynchronous communication tools represent one of the major sources of traffic on the Internet, the expanding variety of real-time communication tools, fueled by the steady increase in bandwidth, promises to have increased impact on Web-based communication in the near future.

Real-time text-based chat has a long and rich history on the pre-Web Internet. Internet Relay Chat (IRC) was developed in 1989, and it has remained a popular tool for people wishing to engage in text-based dialogs. Other text-based chat tools such as ICQ (http://www.icq.com) have gained in popularity recently. While ICQ started out as a simple text chat tool, it is constantly adding new features. For example, ICQ 99a supports real-time text chat as well as e-mail and voice mail. The addition of sound effects with messages is supported, as is file transfers. This merger of capabilities mirrors the evolution of the Web itself. Not surprisingly, tools designed for one function can be enhanced with new features that extend their usability into related areas.

While ICQ started as a tool for desktop computers, it is now reaching into new market spaces. For example, a version exists for the Palm Pilot. This would allow anyone with a wireless modem to engage in text-based chat with people all over the world while sitting on a bus.

The incorporation of video into the real-time chat world became popular years ago when Cornell University released CU-SeeMe, a simple (and primitive) video chat system that used the Internet to convey text-based messages along with video images of the participants. With the recent increase in bandwidth, CU-SeeMe has been expanded to support color images and voice, as well as text-based chat. The product, now commercially available from White Pine Software (http://www.wpine.com), has retained its early ease of use while adding new features to make this a fine tool for simple multi-point video conferences. While the product functions over standard phone lines, videoconferencing quality is inhibited. Quality conferencing, even with small compressed images, requires fast connections. Since my cable modem operates between one and three megabits/second, my transmissions look pretty good as long as I'm connecting to other broadband users. Overall quality is determined by the slowest connection in the loop, so unless everyone in the conference is using broadband connections, quality will suffer.

The synchronous communication tools described so far have counterparts in the physical world. We can (and sometimes do) pass written messages to each other during meetings. We talk over telephones, and we talk face to face so we can see the person with whom we are interacting. The capacity of telematic technologies to support analogs of these physical communication modes is laudable, but Internet-based real-time communication can take on other aspects that have little or no connection to the physical world. These forays into virtual worlds grew out of multiplayer games and science fiction novels.

In Neal Stephenson's 1993 sci-fi novel, *Snow Crash*, for example, the action takes place in two settings: the physical world, and in a virtual world called the Metaverse. Characters bounce between these two worlds as the story progresses. People appear in the Metaverse as images or avatars; their shape can be realistic or generic. They move from place to place under the control of the user, and can engage in conversations with the people they encounter. Documents or other files can be transferred merely by handing them to others (leading to a major problem in the novel).

When *Snow Crash* appeared, I was sure the fictional Metaverse would quickly become reality. With the release of The Palace (http://www.thepalace.com), this prediction came true. The Palace consists of graphical "worlds" containing linked rooms. These worlds can be visited using free client software, or through a Java-enabled browser. Users of the Palace client software can design and use their own avatars.

Palace worlds exist for many topics, and the Palace Web site maintains a list of destinations with information on their current occupancy. Once you visit a Palace, you can move around a room, move to different rooms, and engage in conversation with others you encounter. Messages can be sent to everyone in the room, or "whispered" to individual recipients.

If you don't find a Palace that meets your interests, the company also provides access to a free eight-user server that you can customize with your own room designs and background scripts. The scripting language for the Palace is more complex than HTML, resembling a structured programming language, but simple Palaces can be created without having to master this language because many common options (defining doors and their destinations, for example) are created automatically through some of the built-in room construction tools.

The Palace is one of several virtual worlds to be found on the Internet, and the number of offerings in this area is likely to increase over time.

While the advantage of tools like the Palace may be obvious for social interaction or the creation of adventure games, this software has more serious applications as well. Traditional text-based chat tools are devoid of context — they present a uniform user interface for all topics. The text window in ICQ looks the same if the topic is romance or particle physics. With the Palace, rooms can be designed with pictures and props that provide constant reminders of the subject being discussed. While users are free to chat about anything they wish, the design of a room can help keep conversations on track.

Because of the graphic content, it might seem that the Palace would be more of a bandwidth hog than plain text-based tools like ICQ. To some extent this is true, but the problem is not as great as it first appears. For one thing, users of complex Palaces are usually invited to pre-download all the room graphics at once so that rooms can be rendered on the screen as soon as they are entered. Images for any visited room remain on the user's disk until they are intentionally removed. The movement of the avatar is conveyed through a mouse-click — something that does not require much bandwidth. The rest of the Net traffic is devoted to the textual dialog, allowing the Palace to be used effectively by users with low-bandwidth connections.

The world of on-line Watering Holes is populated with many other tools, and you can spend many hours just exploring the wide variety of synchronous and asynchronous communication tools available for little or no cost.

On-line Watering Holes have interesting properties that come more from the nature of human interaction than from the characteristics of the technologies themselves. Just as Web-based Campfires have rekindled aspects of the manuscript culture in which documents can be shared with interested readers in the absence of a publisher, Web-based Watering Holes rekindle tribal groupings of participants interested in topics that are of interest to a small number of people. The huge number of listservs and newsgroups shows how diverse the interests of Net users are. Sustained dialog on arcane subjects can be facilitated with ease with digital Watering Holes.

While these tools facilitate on-line tribes, these tribes are united through time and interest, not through time and space. One's membership comes not as an accident of birth, but through active choice. Tribes can be entered and left at will, and members of a particular tribe can be dispersed throughout the wide reaches of the Internet itself. (In the past I would have said "world-wide," yet this seemingly expansive description fails to take into account those who will gain access through the International Space Station, or from a colony on Mars sometime in the next forty years.)

While the technologies of synchronous and asynchronous communication tools can support large numbers of users, the optimal size for group interactions is determined by non-technical issues. This is an important point to consider, especially when offering interactive environments as part of an on-line learning project. You might have several hundred students enrolled in a single course. While this does not present much of a challenge for the Campfire portion of the course, group size is a critical issue to consider for Web-based Watering Holes.

Whenever I'm at a large party I find it interesting to see how the group breaks up into small clusters, typically ranging from two to five people. Membership in a cluster changes during the party as people move from one cluster to another. Because the topic of conversation often changes between clusters, people have the chance to take part in several completely different conversations during the course of an evening.

Unmoderated synchronous chat sessions show similar characteristics. After a few people get on-line, subgroups come into existence, each with their own conversational thread. (See, for example, "Communication Conventions in Instructional Electronic Chats," a 1997 *First Monday* article by Karen Murphy and Mauri Collins.) The logistics of keeping up with these threads can intimidate users who lose track of their particular ideas as other topics flash across the screen. For this reason, the optimal size for synchronous chats is probably smaller in unmoderated sessions than it is for topics that are highly structured and have an active moderator. For example, a moderated brainstorming session on naming a new product can be quite effective on-line with a large number of users.

Because chat users often use nick-names and communicate through plain text, relative anonymity can lead to increased willingness to share creative ideas without fear of criticism. As the old cartoon of two dogs sitting in front of a computer said, "On the Internet no one knows you're a dog." Of course the lack of nuance in quickly typed text can lead to misunderstandings that sometimes degenerate into "flame wars," with criticism rapidly ballooning out of hand. This makes the role of the moderator as important on-line as in a physical setting.

Some software (notably CU-SeeMe, the Palace, and other programs using visual images) provide natural limits to group sizes simply because the screen gets too crowded with participants otherwise. In the case of the Palace it is easy to tell a sub-group to move to a vacant room, and to create a new room for this purpose on the fly if needed.

While the issue of group size might seem to be greatest for synchronous communication, it is an issue for asynchronous communication as well. Jacob Palme from Stockholm University has studied this topic (http://www.dsv.su.se/~jpalme/e-mail/group-size.pdf). One of his observations is that there seems to be a minimum size for a listserv, newsgroup, or e-mail-based communication group in order for a conversational thread to be continued. If for example, the likelihood of someone responding to a posting is 5%, then it takes a group size of twenty-one to sustain a dialog. Hot topics with active participants can be sustained with smaller groups, and less engaging topics or groups with passive users need large subscriber bases to maintain a dialog. As with synchronous communication, the presence of a moderator can be helpful in keeping the dialog going, and in keeping people on task.

And so, with Web-based Watering Holes, we encounter either minimum or maximum group sizes depending on whether the communication is asynchronous or synchronous. For designers of Web-based learning environments, this distinction is of critical importance.

Caves

The Cave is the conceptual learning space — the place where information turns into knowledge and wisdom. It is where we generate new ideas and create expressions of them. In the physical world of learning, this space is supported in quiet libraries, kitchen tables, private offices, and other places where we can be alone with our thoughts and the tools needed to create expressions of our insights. In this world we are free to give our thoughts free expression. For students, Cave time is used for the creation of projects, essays, and other creative works. The Cave is home to *Aha!* thinking.

While the Web has numerous tools to facilitate the process of creative expression and concept development, the physical place from which we engage the Web for this task is important as well. If we are trying to concentrate on the development of an idea and there is a lot of distracting noise, our efforts can easily be thwarted. Caves (virtual or otherwise) are places where time can evaporate if we enter a state of flow. This makes Caves hard to accommodate in traditional schools, making it even more important for learners to have access to creative tools outside formal learning environments. To fully take advantage of Cave time, learners need access to the most powerful computer technology available, the best on-line access, and a suite of software that supports creative expression. Clunky software and slow computers can impede access to the flow state. This is why video game consoles often have faster computer chips than those found on most desktop systems.

The critical element is to allow someone to create something without requiring a shift of mental gears to think about the tool. For all the hype surrounding software that is "user friendly," there is precious little on the market that truly meets this objective. The alternative is to spend time in advance becoming proficient with relevant software. For some this will mean mastering a word processing program, while for others it means becoming expert in a high end-graphics package like Adobe Photoshop. There are lots of excellent programs designed to support creative expression through virtually any expressive modality you can imagine — text, images, sounds, animation, video, simulations. To take advantage of these tools in the electronic Cave requires preparation (typically obtained through time spent in the spaces of Campfires and Watering Holes).

Web-based Caves can be thought of as the walls on which our creations are posted, and the act of publishing is as important as the act of creating. It is interesting to observe that more and more applications are including the option to save documents as "Web-ready," or, in some cases, to post the documents to the Web directly. This tendency is a clear expression of the growing importance of the Web as a medium for personal creative expression.

Any attempt to list (let alone describe) the range of software for creative expression would far exceed the scope of this book. Instead, I'll describe a few titles as exemplary Cave tools that can be used in a variety of learning situations. Cave tools fall into two main categories — those for the creation of static documents (images, text, movies) and those for the creation of interactive documents (programs, simulations, etc.). It is fair to ask where traditional Web documents fit into this scheme: Are they static or dynamic documents? The very act of clicking on a hyperlink implies interactivity, yet once you land on a page, you will likely encounter static images or text. In this regard it is fair to say that the Web is a truly hybrid medium, embracing both static and dynamic elements of expression. From the perspective of the Web as a tool for learning, this capability is important. While it is generally accepted that nearly anyone can learn just about anything, each of us has dominant learning modes. Some benefit from reading text, and others from interacting with simulations. Just as this variety of expression is important around the Campfire, it is similarly important when learners express what they know to others as a result of their time in the Cave.

For example, the simplest Web-based Cave expressions are Web pages created and posted by users themselves. Web documents are created using Hypertext Markup Language (HTML) — a "language" for describing the displayed appearance of pages through the use of tags indicating, for example, that certain text is to appear as a heading (usually displayed in larger text than used in the body of a document). Other tags indicate the placement of an image, or mark text that, when clicked on, will cause another Web page to load. Over the past few years, HTML has been extended to include many new tags, each connected with a particular feature. In addition, many Web pages also include sections of "Javascript," a subset of the Java language that is executed directly from within the Web page itself.

While it was common in the early days of the Web for pages to be created by hand with simple text editors, new page authoring tools have been made available to assist in the creation of Web-based documents by whose who find the hand-creation of tags to be tedious. While some professional page creators still fine tune their creations by hand, most rely on professional authoring tools that create HTML in the background, allowing the user to directly build the page or complete Web site in an editor that displays the emerging page as it would appear to an end

131

user. Some of these editing tools, notably Adobe's CyberStudio (http://www.adobe.com) and Roger Wagner's SiteCentral (http://www.sitecentral.com), go out of their way to reduce the barrier between the author's ideas for page design, and the implementation of these ideas.

Generally, Web pages consist of text, static images, and (increasingly) a few special effects such as buttons that change coloring when the mouse is moved over them. Web documents are capable of much more, but the creation of additional objects for pages usually falls outside the scope of most page creation tools. Sounds and movies, for example, are increasing in popularity, especially as users gain access to higher speed connections to the Internet. One of the dominant standards for these media types has been created by Real (http://www.real.com) whose RealAudio and RealVideo standards are supported through free players and inexpensive document creation tools. On the audio front, the MP3 standard has become so popular that, as of July, 1999, MP3 was the most common search term on the Internet (http://www.searchterms.com). MP3 audio files (which approach CD quality at a small fraction of the size) can be created and played back with free software.

Apple Computer's Quicktime 4 (http://quicktime.apple.com) has not only raised the bar on Internet video, it allows movie and MP3 audio files to be played back as they are being loaded into the computer. This feature, called "streaming," means that you can start listening to (or watching) a file before it has been completely transferred to your computer. RealAudio and RealVideo have always supported streaming, but require that the document be loaded through special software, not just read as a simple file uploaded to the Web site.

Web users wishing to gain access to documents using these, or numerous other, special formats can add capability to their browsers through the use of "plug-ins."

In addition to sounds and movies, Real has added support for slide shows that can be viewed over the Web. By using the RealSlideshow software, authors can organize a show consisting of static images with transitions, background music, and narration for each slide. The final show is then compressed for easy playback using the latest RealMedia plug-in.

The majority of authoring tools on the market are geared to the needs of those who want to create documents that will be read, seen, or heard by others. While these modalities encompass much of what we might want to express, the list is by no means complete. For example, a Cave dweller might have an idea that can best be expressed through the creation of a simulation or other program that can be explored by others. While a language (Java) exists expressly for the purpose of creating Web-based programs, the skills needed to master this programming language are quite high. Fortunately, other programming tools exist to support the creation of sophisticated interactive programs, without requiring that the author master the arcane art of programming in Java, C++, or any other text-based programming language. These tools are the programming equivalent of What You See is What You Get (WYSIWYG) page authoring tools — think of them as WYSIWYG programming languages.

Stagecast Creator (http://www.stagecast.com) is a good example of a WYSIWYG programming environment. Unlike traditional programming languages, Creator uses a technique called "programming by demonstration." Instead of writing text to describe the behavior of an object, an object in the simulation is placed in a situation it must handle, and then hand-carried through the situation to its ultimate resolution. The act of directly manipulating the object causes it to acquire a "rule" it will then follow when it encounters the situation again. For example, if you want an object to move across the screen, you set up a "before" and "after" situation showing the location of the object before the rule is activated, and the location afterwards. When the program is run, the object then follows this rule for each tick of the internal clock, causing the object to behave in the manner you demonstrated.

Because each object in the user's microworld can have a large set of rules, a program with several objects can produce quite complex behaviors. In traditional programming languages, this complexity can make debugging quite tedious. From the user's perspective, errors in a Creator simulation are easy to locate and fix since rules are attached to individual objects (or classes of objects) and the offending object can be directly examined (by double-clicking it with the mouse) to see where the problem lies.

This tool also allows completed projects to be saved for distribution over the Web. Because complex systems built in Creator often have very small file sizes, there is no penalty for those who want to replace expository text-based information with interactive programs or multimedia presentations.

Life
Life is the contextual learning space — the space where relevance reigns. It is where we determine the accuracy and appropriateness of information, and apply it to our lives. In the physical world of learning, this space is supported through projects where information is explored for its utility in solving real-world problems. In this world

context, not content is king! For students, Life time is used for the application of their learning in multidisciplinary ways to solve real-world problems. The key words here are rigor *and* relevance.

From the perspective of the Web, Life shows up more in our approach to using the Web than in the details of the content itself. By making our excursions purposeful, and by applying a few guiding principles, we embrace this learning space through a conscious decision to retain a focus on a clearly defined task. This is a tricky skill to master. The Web contains over a billion freely-accessible pages on virtually any topic imaginable. Furthermore, just as in the rest of the expressive media we encounter, the Web contains misinformation. While numerous Web-based search tools exist, there is little guidance provided on the use of these tools for the informal user. In fact, the dominant metaphor for Web access is "surfing," implying that users spend their time skimming along the surface of content skipping from page to page until something catches their eyes. The very design of many Web pages is designed to catch attention as quickly as possible, since every page author is aware that any user is a simple mouse-click away from leaving the site and going somewhere else. In some sense, the very ease of access to information on the Web supports casual "browsing" (another metaphor antithetical to in-depth exploration), rather than intense research and study.

To see how *you* view the Web, answer this question: What site gets accessed when you launch your browser? Do you open with a page related to your Internet service provider (ISP), or the page owned by the company that wrote your browser program? Or, have you set your browser up to open with your favorite search tool? All modern browsers can be set up to open with any page you wish, so the choice is up to you. Your choice might say something about how you view the Web. A page hosted by your ISP might imply that you want them to guide you to points of interest. By starting with a search tool, you are taking matters into your own hands.

While the sheer volume of information on the Web implies benefits beyond those of traditional libraries, the Web is missing the key ingredient that makes libraries so useful: librarians. In particular, the Web does not have librarians who can help you focus your search and ask questions to guide you toward the information you want. I didn't realize the tremendous value of research librarians until I started working at the Xerox Palo Alto Research Center (PARC), where I was blessed to connect with Dr. Guliana Lavendel — a librarian's librarian. Guliana taught me how to conduct library research on highly technical subjects, even though the content area of these topics was well outside her field of expertise. I have changed professional interests several times since working at PARC, yet the skills I learned from Dr. Lavendel continue to be relevant today.

While my own use of the Web is (largely) highly focused, I often encounter people who have little idea how to use the Web effectively. This problem is compounded when young children are provided with Web access in school. Time is at a premium in our classrooms, and it is tragic to see youngsters getting lost in cyberspace in their quest for information they need for a project.

In response to this challenge, I strongly believe that every user of the Web should make a concerted effort to master three foundational skills:

- Finding information
- Determining relevance
- Assessing accuracy

While I believe these skills are essential for using any informational repository (including physical libraries), they are even more essential in the world of the Web where we are unlikely to have the ongoing advice of a research librarian available to us. While a full treatment of these skills deserves its own book, I will provide a few suggestions as starting points.

The first step in developing these three Life skills involves knowing how to find information in the first place. In the early days of the Web, documents could be found using two different tools: search engines and directories.

Search engines operate by gathering information from Web sites using a software "spider" that crawls through the Web, building an index of words contained on each site it encounters. When a user types in a request for information, the words in the user's request are matched against a directory of searched sites and a list is generated with the locations of the pages that have been identified as containing these words. While the user may think he or she is "searching the Web," this is not the case. The search is of a directory built by the search engine itself. Because of this limitation, different search engines may produce strikingly different results for a search. For this reason, active Web searchers experiment with different search engines, and develop special strategies for getting the best out of each search tool they use. Some search engines encourage users to type in their request in plain English. Others work best when Boolean logic is used. It is important to note, however, that no search engine claims to have a complete map of the Web. This means that, no matter how many relevant responses you receive, there is a strong likelihood that additional relevant information is available for you on the Web, but that you won't find it using these tools.

Directories are even more incomplete than search engines, but they have an advantage: they are created by hand as linked lists of sites whose content (usually) is both germane and reliable. The first popular directory was Yahoo! (http://www.yahoo.com), and the work of the people who created this directory paid off in Yahoo's incredible popularity.

One advantage of directories is that they provide a context for information. Related sites are clustered under the same heading. This makes directories valuable starting points for research. It is often the case that sites listed in a directory also provide links to other relevant sites, expanding the information base. But these links have a bias driven by the interests of the author of the page. For this reason, directories co-exist easily with search engines.

The blending of these two approaches to finding information on the Web is now so complete that almost every directory also supports Web searching, and almost every search engine also has a directory of hand-picked sites covering a wide range of topics.

Before leaving this topic, there is another category of search tool that has become quite popular: the "metasearch" engine. For example, Dogpile (http://www.dogpile.com) allows you to simultaneously conduct a search on eleven search engines. It also supports the searching of newsgroups, ftp sites, and other places where information may be stored on the Internet. One recent entry to this field is Ask Jeeves (http://www.askjeeves.com) — a metasearch tool that encourages users to ask questions in plain English. In conducting its search, it often rephrases the question based on information it has found, and then presents you with a list of questions (usually related) for which it did find answers. By selecting any of these new questions, the user is taken directly to a relevant site. Unlike Dogpile, Ask Jeeves hides site locations until you have drilled down to the response you want. This makes it a very valuable tool for those who are new to the Web, or for those looking for single answers to well-defined questions.

The issue of relevance can be handled (in part) by how a search is conducted. Searches that are too broad produce thousands of results, only a few of which are likely to be of value. The time wasted looking at irrelevant material can be a major source of frustration for anyone doing research on the Web. For this reason, you might think that it would be wonderful if you conducted a search and every item that was returned was relevant to your work. While this list is of great value, you need to be careful if everything you find is germane. In all likelihood you limited the scope of your search too much, and you are missing other relevant material that would have been found if you'd expanded the scope of your search a bit. There is no hard rule, but you are probably conducting a search pretty well if the number of irrelevant responses is about ten percent of the total.

One strategy for narrowing searches that works with most search engines is to start with a broad search producing thousands of responses. Then, using your search engine's advanced search tools, refine your search from within this master list. Successive refinements should be examined for relevance, and you should feel comfortable stopping when every page of results has at least one or two completely irrelevant results.

While technology can be of tremendous help in the area of relevance, the issue of accuracy falls squarely in the human domain. The criteria you apply to Web pages should be the same ones you use when evaluating the veracity of any information you receive. Unfortunately, many people lack the skills needed to separate fact from fiction. A quick scan of the "newspaper" headlines at a supermarket checkout stand shows how willing people are to accept fiction as fact. Many people believe that anything in print (or from a computer) is accurate. The same blind acceptance of information applies when it is delivered over the radio or television.

While there are probably many reasons for people's blind acceptance of information as truth, one compelling reason can probably be traced to the reliance of schools on textbooks. From an early age, students are taught to believe what they see in textbooks — in fact they are even tested on this material. As a consequence, memory replaces thought. The book says it is so, and therefore it must be. Of course many textbooks contain numerous errors of omission and commission. Relevant and accurate information germane to a topic may be left out of a textbook because it is controversial, and the publisher does not want to take a chance on losing a state-wide contract. Other information is just plain wrong — either because the authors made a mistake, or because new information became available after the book was printed. Because science textbooks (for example) are used for five to seven years before being replaced, they are particularly susceptible to obsolescence during their life cycle.

An alternative is to make more use of original source material in education. In the past this was prohibitively expensive to do, since these materials were not widely available. But now, many collections of historical source material have been made available on the Web. And virtually everything discovered or thought about in the past decade has a Web site or two devoted to it. The problem with raw source material is that it often lacks context or connection to other related material. For example, sites devoted to Impressionist paintings are unlikely to provide in-depth coverage of the music of the period, even though this connection is worth making. Second, some of the source material may be inaccurate or biased. Unless you have been taught how to make connections between information, and taught to find ways to verify the accuracy of information, your work is compromised. These skills can be taught, and they should be part of the basic curriculum for everyone living, working or learning in the coming years.

Unless we address the three issues of finding information, determining relevance, and assessing accuracy, the Life space of the Web will have failed to live up to its potential.

And so, for now, we conclude our exploration of Campfires, Watering Holes, Caves and Life on the Web. As we move on to the final chapter of this book, it is important for you to keep in mind the fact that the Web is changing daily — growing both in content and capability. As you explore the role of the Web as a tool for learning, be on the lookout for new ways the Web can resonate with the four primordial learning spaces. The story has started, but it is far from ending.

The Tetrad Revisited

The major goal of this book has been to explore the Web's potential as an educational tool. Toward that end I've spent a lot of time exploring the metaphors of four primordial learning spaces: Campfires, Watering Holes, Caves, and Life. The insights gained from exploring these spaces will help as we revisit McLuhan's Laws of Media to answer his four questions. The answers to these questions are important for anyone interested in using the Web as a learning tool that moves beyond its early stages as a tool for distance learning. The dynamic nature of the Web insures that the answers I'm sharing are incomplete. I hope you will expand on them yourself and share your insights with me through e-mail (DThornburg@aol.com).

The remainder of this chapter is devoted to answering four essential questions:

- What does the Web enhance?
- What does it obsolete?
- What does it rekindle from the past?
- What does it flip into when pushed to the limit?

What does the Web enhance?

Access to original source material
As the rich digital collections found at the Library of Congress and elsewhere attest, the Web is expanding access to materials that were once only available to researchers under very restricted conditions. Second or third-hand quotations from historical documents can now be replaced by access to the documents in their entirety. The value of this is multifold. First, quotes in textbooks or other compendia are generally extracted out of context to reinforce a singular point of view: that of the book's author. By experiencing a digital copy of the original document, you are free to gain independent insights on the meaning of the work.

Anywhere/anytime learning
Schools (in the United States) are generally in session for 180 days, six periods a day. Brainstorms or insights on academic work that come outside that time frame have little chance for development in the traditional brick-based school. The Web facilitates access to informational sources and conversations with peers and experts virtually any time of the day or night. Furthermore, when the tools of access and creative expression are owned by the learner, they can be used wherever the learner happens to be. This "anywhere" aspect of Web-based learning will gain in popularity as low-cost highly portable Internet appliances become commonplace in the coming years.

Lifelong learning
Unlike traditional colleges in which you make the transition from student to potential donor on graduation, Web-based learning is available to all who want to use it, for as long as they wish. While many Web-based courses are being offered through traditional educational institutions, the rise of true virtual schools based on lifelong

learning will happen soon. These institutions will understand the diverse needs of their users, and respond to these needs in ways that take advantage of the unique features of the Web. While this path is also open to traditional brick-based schools, most of them will fail to see the opportunity until it is too late.

Multiple learning modalities and styles
While some traditional classrooms are making the transition from whiteboards to multimedia projection systems, the Web has embraced multimedia almost since its inception. It was its capacity to display various media types (not just text) that catapulted the Web into public awareness. Multimedia supports a wide variety of learning styles far better than an educational system devoted primarily to the representation of ideas only through text and numbers. When learners are freed to express what they know in ways that are natural to them (such as video, sounds, animations, simulations, images, *and* text and numbers), learning improves.

Contextual learning
Contextual learning can (and does) take place in many classrooms, but the overall curriculum is largely driven by abstract standards that treat knowledge as separable into neat departmentalized categories broken down by age appropriateness. There may be merit to this approach, but when taken to the extreme it breeds a community of learners who ask, "Why do I need to know this?" only to be told: "Because it will be on the test." With the Web, context can be a driving force for exploration simply because information is so abundant that it becomes meaningless without the contextual connection.

Global awareness
The Web's reach expands to the planet (and, soon, beyond). Anyone with Web access in any country can

gain access to information and peers virtually anywhere else. While the United States (and English) dominate Web sites today, the increasingly rapid growth of sites reflecting the language and cultures of other countries is turning the Web into an international bazaar of ideas.

Creative expression
Virtually all Internet service providers set aside storage space so users can post their own Web sites. Other companies (such as Yahoo) do the same for anyone gaining access to the Web. This affords the opportunity for learners to share their insights globally. While a brick-based school is often decorated with student work posted on classroom walls, the audience (and impact) is local. By posting creative expressions on the Web, the potential for feedback and collaboration is expanded almost beyond comprehension.

What does the Web obsolete?

Textbooks
Textbooks perpetuate the blind acceptance of printed information, even though they are often used long after some of their content has become obsolete. Because textbooks are generally written so as to offend as few people as possible, challenging topics or points of view are often hidden from learners. These limitations are removed when information is obtained through reputable sources on the Web. Information in fast-moving fields (such as astronomy, genetics, etc.) is disseminated rapidly — usually for free. Of course (as in previous expressive media) there is at least as much incorrect information as correct information on the Web, providing an opportunity for users to develop the skills of discrimination needed to separate the wheat from the chaff of cyberspace.

Dry lectures and lecturers

The teacher as sole provider of knowledge disappears when learners have access to the Web. Access to the thoughts of numerous experts in almost any field can be obtained with ease. The teacher droning on, chalk in hand, could count on threat or social pressure to keep students in their seats, no matter how little they were learning, nor how bored they were getting with the content. Because learning about a subject is connected to learning the teacher's attitudes about the subject, boring educators have done a disservice to students. Like much of life, teaching is a performing art — enthusiasm and authenticity are powerful tools, and we all have stories of teachers who (for better or worse) shaped our view of their subject not by what they said, but by how they said it.

The Web provides a powerful showcase for those educators who truly love their subject, and who can now share that love with a global audience. Through the Web, virtually any subject can be explored through the perspective of educators who truly understand and treasure their topics. Because the relative anonymity of the Web-based leaner permits it, boring educators will be abandoned with a single mouse click.

Rote learning and the bulimic curriculum

The traditional curriculum in many schools looks like a cross between *Jeopardy*, and *I've Got a Secret*. The first of these games refers to the quest for memorizing fragmented clips of knowledge to be fed back on a test (and then forgotten as quickly as possible). The second represents the perspective of some educators that information is to be metered out to students and even withheld if it is not deemed appropriate for students to know it: "You'll learn about that *next* year."

With the Web, these games become obsolete. Learners are free to develop the big picture — to look at learning from a systemic perspective in which various topics are linked to each other. This, in fact, was the driving force behind Vannevar Bush's invention of the concept of hypertext in the 1940's. The binge and purge model of learning is, with the Web, replaced by the building of learning from a solid foundation that continues to be developed and expanded over the years.

Linear monomedia expressions as sole representation of student learning

The traditional ten-page written report is obsoleted as the sole method for student expression when the multimedia aspects of the Web are embraced by learners as authors. The Web not only supports a wide variety of media types, it also supports associative linking through which authors can create documents that can be perused in a non-linear fashion. This allows the recipient of a document to examine it in unique ways based on interest or preferred representational styles. Documents created with this intent in mind have no printed counterpart. These documents are interactive verbs, not static nouns.

Top-down information delivery

Traditional educational practice is hierarchical in design. At the top is the State mandated curriculum and the tests that measure student achievement. At the next level down, the publishers explore the source material and create textbooks designed to support this curriculum. Next, the teachers convey content to the students and administer the tests. And, finally, the student is at the bottom of the ladder as the recipient of content over which she has no control. In this model context is irrelevant. The determination of what is to be taught is made at layers outside the control of the teachers or learners and passed down as mandates. New information

148

relating to pedagogical methods or corrections to content must wait until the state decides to revisit the curriculum — typically in five to seven year cycles.

This model is obsoleted with the Web. Textbook publishers are disintermediated because the Web allows easy access to the source material itself. Teachers and learners can become collaborators, and students become publishers as they disseminate the results of their studies to a global audience of peers.

What does the Web rekindle?

Manuscript culture
The Web rekindles the manuscript culture that dominated the period prior to the development of the mass-produced book. In this model, a few copies of manuscripts were disseminated among a small circle of interested readers who then made copies for themselves if they wished. The low barrier to publishing on the Web and the ease with which document formats such as Adobe Acrobat (pdf files) can be viewed on virtually any computer platform insures that documents can easily be shared among a circle of interested readers. The difference, of course, is that the reach of the Web is global, the time lag for distribution has vanished, and copies can be made in seconds. Early drafts of this book were disseminated to a small circle of readers in this fashion before it was sent to the printer. I distribute many articles of mine that have never been published except on the Web. (See http://www.pbs.org/thornburg and http://www.tcpd.org for examples.)

Electronic tribes
The Web rekindles membership in tribes — social organizations reaching back thousands of years. While membership in a physical tribe is usually an accident of

birth, electronic tribal membership is based on common interests, not geography. Newsgroups and listservs are two examples of tribal structures, and chat rooms and Web-based conferences are others. Members are free to join as many tribes as they wish, and to leave tribes when they no longer meet the needs of the participant.

Painting on the walls of digital caves
Expressions painted on the walls of caves provided opportunities for the artist and viewer alike to explore the dynamism of life in frozen form. The quest for expressive freedom and pride of authorship has been with us ever since. In the physical world, today's urban cave painters use spray paint to tag walls. The potential viewership of wall-based art pales in comparison with that possible for art posted on the walls of digital caves. Through the use of free page-hosting services, artists are free to share their work with a viewing audience worldwide.

In addition to static works of art, other media of creative expression are supported by the Web as well. Musical compositions, animations, movies, simulations — all these and more can be posted with the same ease as posting a poem or painting.

Thinking
Before the scribes developed formal educational institutions, humans needed to think to survive. Once textbooks became commonplace, memorization became a dominant task of learners. The content of the book was not questioned, it was merely committed to memory so it could be fed back on a test. In the time of Socrates, memorization was not as dominant a tool for learning as it later became. Prior to writing, there was no "original" against which the memory could be tested, and thinking was an important skill.

The Web rekindles thinking for several reasons. First the scope of its content is so large, and is changing so rapidly, that memorization is physically impossible. Second, because fact is commingled with fiction, Web users need to develop thinking skills in order to assess the relevance and accuracy of what they find.

Learning as doing

The interactivity of the Web rekindles learning by doing — a dominant strategy for pre-literate cultures. The active engagement of the learner increases the likelihood that what is learned will be both remembered and used. Stone masons learned their craft from masters who taught them through demonstration and example. All learning in the guilds was contextual — nothing was learned without the expectation of application. The rich interactivity of the Web coupled with the ease with which users can post their own work conspires to bring context back to the forefront through the concrete application of ideas and their demonstration and expansion at the hands of the learners themselves.

What does the Web flip into when pushed to the limit?

Learner centered education

Unlike television, radio, or school, the Web is truly a user-centered medium. The user determines which pages to visit, which links to click on any page, and even how to view a particular site. Early attempts to use the Web as an educational tool have tried to preserve the school-based structure in which the teacher determines the pace, content, and structure of a course. This will change in the future simply because this approach is antithetical to the core nature of the Web. In the new model the educator may be replaced by a learning coach who collaborates with learners to help them formulate a plan for acquiring the skills they need or desire. The transformation from educator to on-line coach will be as great as the transformation in education that took place with the wide distribution of mass-produced books.

Learning constant, time variable
As Web-based learning environments become more commonplace, they will shed some of the remaining vestiges of brick-based institutions for which time is a constant and learning is a variable. With the Web there is no reason for any course to demand anything less than excellence from its learners, providing them with as much time and support as needed to achieve this level of performance. This means that the only grades a learner can receive are "excellent," or "incomplete." Some learners will progress quickly through a course of study, and others will need more time to establish mastery. Web-based courses based on brick-based schools have failed to grasp this simple fact: we each learn at different rates. As a result, they hold time constant and let the grades fall where they may. As this model changes, we will look back on our current educational model with the same emotions that we contemplate what operations must have been like prior to the discovery of anesthetics.

Distinction between learning and work
Taken to the limit, the anywhere/anytime aspect of Web-based learning will blur the distinctions between learning and work. The old model of school/work/retirement will disappear as people use the new technologies as tools to keep their minds alive and growing throughout their lifetimes. This will be important for at least two reasons. First, the average life span is increasing, and many people are remaining in the workforce long past the traditional time for retirement. Second, the dynamic nature of the economy has produced tremendous shifts in jobs, with some jobs disappearing forever while new jobs (requiring

new skills) appear on the horizon. It is difficult to imagine any job in the future that will not require continuous learning on the part of workers. Learning will increasingly become embedded in the work itself, and the Web will evolve into a dominant tool for this activity.

Replacement of information with creativity as a dominant paradigm

The late twentieth century has been called the Information Age because the dominant economic forces have shifted from industrial production to knowledge work. The past fifty years have been marked by an exponential growth of information, yet this is merely the continuation of a process that has been going on for centuries. What makes the past fifty years significant is not the rate of information growth, but the fact that our access to information has grown exponentially. In recent years, the Web has played an important role in increasing our access to information. The combination of ever increasing information and ever increasing access has resulted in infoglut of epidemic proportions. We have flipped information access from a rarity to a cheap commodity. Content is no longer king; context is.

Because of this, learning will no longer be about information, it will be about creativity: learning how to access the information as it is needed, and then applying this information in highly contextualized fashion in increasingly creative ways. If success in the twentieth century was based on what you knew, success in the new century will be based on what you can create.

Some final thoughts...

This has been my most philosophical book to date, yet I think it has the potential to be the most practical one I have ever written. Futurists are generally technologists, demographers, or economists. As a technologist I think I have the trickiest task. The foundation on which my work is based is constantly changing. In this environment, predictions or insights of long-term value are hard to come by because the tools and techniques of technology undergo constant development. Fortunately, the affect and effect of expressive media have consequences that transcend the ever-changing landscape of the media themselves. If it is the case that the medium is the message (as McLuhan taught), then a productive way to explore media types is through the messages they carry. That has been my approach in the book, and it is one I hope will allow the ideas expressed here to remain relevant for years to come.

Beyond that, there is another point: If the medium is the message, then we have the opportunity to define media through the messages we wish to communicate. The reluctance of some educators to embrace technologies like the Web reflects a deep understanding of this principle. The message they wish to communicate (the hierarchical delivery of metered information) is antithetical to the flattened information space of the Web. The challenge is not that these folks don't understand technology — in fact they understand its power all too well. Like the scribes who lost power with the advent of the mass-produced book, these educators will hold on to what power remains in the typographic culture, and petition their institutions to avoid change at all costs.

The problem is that, with the Web, learners increasingly have the opportunity to take things into their own hands. The debate on the utility of technology in education will continue to take place for years to come. My guess, though, is that this debate will take place outside of educational institutions — perhaps echoing through the halls of old school buildings vacated because they failed to meet the needs of twenty-first century learners.

Another challenge we face involves equity of access. As numerous studies (such as the 1999 report *Falling Through the Net: Defining the Digital Divide* from the U. S. Department of Commerce) have confirmed, the gap between the access rich and access poor is widening along lines of race, income, and geographical location. Unless dynamic measures are taken to reverse this trend, we risk the creation of a permanent underclass in a society where information technologies are increasingly important tools for learners and workers alike.

My hope, dear reader, is that you have found enough in these pages to help you think about telematic tools for education in productive new ways. The challenge to transform education is tremendous, but it is the most worthwhile gift we can give the next generation.

References

Becker, Henry, *Internet Use by Teachers: Conditions of Professional Use and Teacher-Directed Student Use*, http://www.crito.uci.edu/TLC/findings/Internet-Use/startpage.htm, 1999.

Csikszentmihalyi, Mihaly, *Creativity: Flow and the Psychology of Discovery and Invention*, Harper Collins, 1996.

Gardner, Howard, *Frames of Mind: The Theory of Multiple Intelligences*, Basic Books, 1983.

Hawthorne, Nathaniel, *House of the Seven Gables*, http://sailor.gutenberg.org/gutenberg/

Hiltz, Starr Roxanne, and Turoff, Murray, *The Network Nation: Human Communication Via Computer*, Addison-Wesley, 1978.

Hugo, Victor, *The Hunchback of Notre Dame*, Modern Library, 1941.

Innis, Harold, *Empire and Communications*, Press Porcépic, 1986.

Innis, Harold, *The Bias of Communication*, University of Toronto Press, 1951.

Irving, Larry, *Falling Through the Net: Defining the Digital Divide*, U.S. Department of Commerce, http://www.ntia.doc.gov, 1999.

Kaipa, Prasad, *Pyramids*, http://mithya.com/pyramids/

Kao, John, *Jamming: The Art and Discipline of Business Creativity*, HarperBusiness, 1997.

Kehoe, Colleen, et al., *GVU 10th WWW User Survey*, http://www.gvu.gatech.edu/user_surveys/survey-1998-10),1998.

Levinson, Paul, *Digital McLuhan: A Guide to the Information Millenium*, Routledge, 1999.

McLuhan, Eric, *Electric Language: Understanding the Message*, St. Martins, 1998.

McLuhan, Marshall and Eric, *Laws of Media: The New Science*, University of Toronto Press, 1988.

McLuhan, Marshall, and Powers, Bruce R., *The Global Village: Transformations in World Life and Media in the 21st Century*, Oxford University Press, 1989.

McLuhan, Marshall, *The Gutenberg Galaxy: The Making of Typographic Man*, University of Toronto Press, 1962.

McLuhan, Marshall, *Understanding Media: The Extensions of Man*, McGraw-Hill, 1964.

Murphy, Karen, and Collins, Mauri, "Communication Conventions in Instructional Electronic Chats," *First Monday*, http://www.firstmonday.dk/issues/issue2_11/murphy/, 1997.

Murray, Janet, *Hamlet on the Holodeck:The Future of Narrative in Cyberspace*, Free Press, 1997.

Nelson, Mark, *We Have the Information You Want, But Getting It Will Cost You: Being Held Hostage by Information Overload*, http://www.acm.org/crossroads/xrds1-1/mnelson.html, 1994.

O'Donnell, James, *Avatars of the Word: From Papyrus to Cyberspace*, Harvard University Press, 1998.

Palme, Jacob, The Optimal Group Size in Computer Mediated Communication, http://www.dsv.su.se/~jpalme/e-mail/group-size.pdf, 1995.

Plato, *Phaedrus*, http://sailor.gutenberg.org/gutenberg/

Stephenson, Neal, *Snow Crash*, Bantam Books, 1993.

Toffler, Alvin, *The Third Wave*, Morrow, 1980.

Woolley, David, *The Future of Web Conferencing*, http:thinkofit.com/webcon/ wcfuture.htm, 1998.

Web Sites

The following is an alphabetical list of the sites referenced in this book. All site addresses were current at the time of publication. Periodic updates will be available at the Thornburg Center site: http://www.tcpd.org

http://awsd.com/scripts/webbbs   Source for Web conferencing program

http://education.nasa.gov   NASA educational site

http://learn.ivv.nasa.gov   Another NASA educational site

http://memory.loc.gov   Library of Congress American Memory Project

http://memory.loc.gov/ammem/bellhtml/bellhome.html Alexander Graham Bell collected writings

http://memory.loc.gov/ammem/edhtml/ edhome.html Thomas Edison recordings site

http://millennium.aed.org   AED dialog on educational technology

http://netmail.web.aol.com Site for America Online users to check their mail from public terminals without AOL client

http://quicktime.apple.com   Source for Quicktime software

http://spacelink.nasa.gov Main NASA educational site

http://spacelink.nasa.gov/Instructional.Materials/
Curriculum.Support NASA teacher support
http://thinkofit.com/webcon/wcfuture.htm   David
Woolley paper on Web conferencing
http://tile.net/lists List of active listservs
http://www.adobe.com   Source for demo version of
CyberStudio and other Adobe products
http://www.askjeeves.com Popular metasearch site using
natural language
http://www.crito.uci.edu/TLC Becker study on Internet
use
http://www.dogpile.com Popular metasearch site
http://www.download.com Source for shareware
http://www.dsv.su.se/~jpalme/e-mail/group-size.pdf Jacob
Palme article on the effect of group size on
asynchronous communication
http://www.ed.gov/free U.S. Dept. of Education project
directory
http://www.eudora.com Site for Eudora e-mail program
http://www.gvu.gatech.edu/user_surveys/survey-1998-10
Georgia Tech Web user survey
http://www.hotmail. com Free e-mail service
http://www.icq.com Source for ICQ chat software
http://www.isoc.org/guest/zakon/Internet/History/HIT.html
Hobbes' Internet Timeline
http://www.mailstartplus.com   Site for checking e-mail
from public terminals
http://www.mars2030.net Mars Millenium Project site
http://www.mithya.com
http://www.nasa.gov Main NASA site
http://www.pbs.org/thornburg   Monthly PBS audio
program by D. Thornburg
http://www.real.com   Source for RealAudio and other
products from Real
http://www.searchterms.com   Site for finding the most
popular search terms

http://www.sitecentral.com   Source for demo of SiteCentral Web authoring software

http://www.ssec.wisc.edu Cloud image database

http://www.stagecast.com Source for Stagecast Creator software

http://www.sun.com/sunergy   Sun Microsystems educational site

http://www.tcpd.org Thornburg Center Web Site

http://www.thegateway.org GEM project site

http://www.thepalace.com Source for The Palace client and server software

http://www.wdatai.com World Data Interactive site

http://www.wpine.com   Source for CU-SeeMe video conferencing software

http://www.yahoo.com Popular search site

Other recent books by David Thornburg

Brainstorms and Lightning Bolts: Thinking Skills for the Twenty-first Century, Starsong Publications, 1998.

Putting the Web to Work: Transforming Education for the Next Century, Starsong Publications, 1996.

Education in the Communication Age, Starsong Publications, 1993.

To order any of these books, to secure consulting services, or to have Dr. Thornburg make a presentation to your conference or organization, contact:

The Thornburg Center
P.O. Box 7168
San Carlos, CA 94070
United States of America

1-650-508-0314

dthornburg@aol.com

http://www.tcpd.org